Featured Creatures
Animals in our lives

By Lalita Gandbhir

© Copyright 2022 Lalita Gandbhir

Email: lalitagandbhir@gmail.com

https://www.facebook.com/lalitaGandbhirBooks/

No parts of this publication may be reproduced by any means without the express written permission of the author.

ISBN: 978-1-7338357-9-4

Cover illustration/design and interior drawings by Amit Kaikini

*Dedicated to all creatures that walk,
jump, crawl, creep, swim and fly*

Contents

Foreword

Before marriage, I never considered the Animal Factor. By that, I mean the issue of love for animals. My husband, Sharad, loves animals. He likes them in his yard, in the living room, on his sofas, on his lap, in his kitchen, on the kitchen countertops, and in his bed. He plays with them, teases them, and pets them. He is fine with them in the backseat of the car, breathing down the necks of the people in front.

My husband spent several years of his childhood in small Indian towns surrounded by jungle. He was a wild, mischievous, fearless, and naughty boy, and he had many common pets, as well as chickens and water buffalo. His childhood adventures involving his animals are family legends. His mother wrote about them and told those stories to our children, who now entertain their own children with them. In this book, I've included an article about his childhood experiences with animals, so that readers can understand his background.

Unlike my husband, I was raised in a city. And I don't like pets at all. I prefer not to have any. I don't like their barking or the other noises they make, or the hair they shed. I don't like cleaning up their kitty litter, or having to take dogs for walks and clean up their droppings. I don't understand why people unnecessarily complicate their lives. I can tolerate them in the backyard or on our living room floor, as long as I don't have to be responsible for them.

I am sure by now that you can see the conflict.

For the first few years of our married life, we couldn't afford any pets, so there was no disagreement on the subject.

Then we bought a house and had a daughter named Veena. When she was three years old, she demanded a cat. She asked for a cat every day, and she chased after cats in the neighborhood. Eventually, a kitten entered our life. It had been easy to deny a pet to my husband, but I found it difficult to deny one to my daughter. My husband claimed that if children don't have pets, their brains become damaged, and that denying a pet to a child is child abuse. I doubted his statements. In fact, the dog we had when I was a child had traumatized me. Still, we got a cat.

Then our second daughter, Neena, was born. Her older sister loved the new addition but didn't consider her a pet substitute.

Much later we had a son, Raj. All three children loved animals. Pets paraded into our lives.

Now I have grandchildren who also all love animals. I have decided that there must be a dominant Animal Love gene.

My husband and children claim that there is an "animal sense." Along with our five senses, this is a sixth. People who have it can read animals' minds. They instinctively know what a dog, cat, or any other pet — like a snake or gecko — is thinking. They can even sense what wild animals think.

Tomya, the unpredictable family dog that I grew up with, may be the reason I don't like pets. But I do like to watch wild animals: birds, snakes, spiders — all wildlife. I consider wildlife a part of nature. And since I love nature, I love wildlife.

Because of my family, I have had a succession of pets imported into my life, with or without my consent. *With* my consent, we've visited many wildlife parks, and observed animals in the wild. In this book I am including only those wildlife encounters that are imprinted in my memory.

This is a story of the pets that lived with us and the wildlife that briefly featured in our lives. All these animals — even the ones I resisted — have made my life colorful and interesting. This book is devoted to the animal world.

In past years, I've written stories about our children's pets in Marathi and have had them published in Marathi magazines like *Ekata* in Toronto and in Marathi magazines in India. Some of these stories I wrote recently, others I wrote years back, which is why they reflect different time periods in my life. My grandchildren have heard all these stories.

This book is also a family legacy.

Part One
Wild Creatures

Chapter 1
Wildlife in my little world

Behind our house is an eight-acre playground that's full of life. Around its circular perimeter are homes, tennis courts, and what was once a school, but is now a senior apartment complex. The playground is surrounded by a chain-link fence. The town owns and maintains the playground. According to rumor, it was once a lake. Back when nature was plentiful, the owner filled it in and donated it to the town, along with the adjacent land, to build a school.

Bunny in yard (photo by Sage Stossel)

A ten-foot-wide dirt and grass road leads from our street to the playground. A few narrow dirt paths also lead to it. Only feet or bicycles can travel over those paths. When the road is muddy or snow-covered, only feet can walk to the playground.

Approximately half a mile from our house is a lake, surrounded by graceful old homes. The area is classified as historic. The town has preserved old-fashioned gas lights on the road around the lake.

The town has also reserved part of the lakeshore for townspeople to swim. That portion of the shore has a beach with stalls for changing and washing. Other parts of the lakeshore have benches, where people relax or play with their dogs.

On the opposite side, are streetcar tracks, over which streetcars periodically run. A walkway encircles half the lake.

Since we moved into our house, I have been observing the playground from the back window of our kitchen and the back deck of the house. I watch the creatures that live there, and the ones that come and go, or pay seasonal visits. Their lives and activities are closely tied to the seasons.

I have also made it a habit to walk around the lake once a day. Both creatures and humans ignore me, which I like. That way, they can be themselves, while I watch them unseen.

In the winter, the playground is white with snow, and the trees are leafless. I can see activity on the playground clearly. If the snow isn't too deep, dog owners in boots walk their dogs on the playground. Most of the time the dogs know each other, and they play. Their owners gather together and talk. Sometimes dogs fight, and their owners struggle to separate them. Children also use the playground, playing in the snow. If the snow is fresh, a few cross-country skiers circle the perimeter. On one side of the playground is a low hill. Children sled down it. Parents in hats, boots, and mittens, watch them and talk.

There are other animals, too. Cats can be seen running around. And there are mice that live in burrows in the ground. I don't see them, but they make their presence known when they come into our house on cold days. Mouse droppings, usually in the kitchen, announce their presence.

"Don't kill the mouse! Don't set the traps!" the girls beg. Neena can catch mice and put them in a bottle. She then sets them free on the playground. But the next day, the mouse is right back. Not wanting to kill the mice, I have called pest control and asked how can I mouse-proof the house. They reply that a mouse can enter a home through a hole the size of a dime. That means our 100-year-old Victorian house cannot be mouse-proofed. I have to get rid of the mice. So I set traps.

Most birds migrate. But the sparrows stick around. They try to pick who knows what out of the snow. I throw rice out into the backyard for them. But that's not enough. I don't know what they eat, but they survive the winter.

I try to walk around the lake. The walkway is never shoveled. The snow has to melt before I can do it. When I do manage to walk around the lake in deep winter, I see the partially frozen lake surrounded by leafless trees, the empty beach, and benches covered with snow. Sometimes a duck or two floats in the water. That's the only sign of life.

Occasionally the lake freezes, and the town erects a sign saying, "No skating." The lake never freezes enough to make skating safe.

Everyone thinks winter is almost over when the weather starts to warm up. But then, unexpectedly, freezing rain falls. It covers the world with a thin, transparent, glass-like sheen that reflects the sunlight. I see birds and outdoor cats shivering in the frozen world. The ice doesn't last very long, though. It melts soon, because the weather warms up again.

When the snow melts, the playground turns into the lake it once was. A few brave souls still walk their dogs there. Both dogs and owners get soaking wet, but they don't care. A few children go there, too, and run around laughing. Seagulls appear from nowhere and dive in to catch nonexistent fish. Wearing boots, I have walked into the water to see what the gulls are trying to catch, and have found nothing. To my surprise, once in in a while I have seen egrets, and even a blue heron.

Eventually, the water evaporates, and the playground is muddy. The dog walkers give up, and walk their dogs on the road. A few children run into the mud and come out completely covered. I have occasionally seen a dog enjoy a mud bath. Later on, the angry owner washes the dog with a hose. The poor dog has to tolerate the spray of cold water.

Eventually, the mud on the playground dries, and delicate green grass starts to sprout. A couple of weeks later, the playground turns green and comes to life with visitors.

Soon municipal trucks arrive, and men draw white lines for games. Little League and Big League baseball, soccer, and other games start.

The playground is full. The dog walkers are forced to walk on the periphery.

When the ice that covered the lake melts, and the walkway around it is free of snow, I walk around the lake every day. A few ducks return to the water. And if I'm lucky, I see little turtles swimming, or sunning themselves on the roots of the trees that grow into the lake.

Spring ducklings (photo by Sage Stossel)

A woodpecker pecking a tree wakes us up with its tapping noise, and we know spring has arrived. After the woodpecker, robins appear on the budding trees. Blue jays and mockingbirds follow.

A mockingbird sings, and my husband Sharad whistles. The mockingbird whistles back. The children laugh and ask their dad to whistle again and again.

Flocks of migrating birds arrive, and rest for a night or two in the neighborhood trees. Among them are large numbers of blackbirds. They settle into a tree. Sharad stands under it and claps. Hundreds of them fly up off the branches, into the sky. Then they come back and settle down onto the tree again.

On moonlit nights, I watch V-shaped formations of wild geese flying. For me it is a thrilling experience.

In the corner between our kitchen and the back deck is a rain gutter attached to the sloping roof. Every year, a few sparrows try to build a nest there. The first time they built the nest, we let them. We had to constantly sweep the corner underneath, because the birds dropped sticks, leaves, and other things they had collected to build the nest. It was a mistake. When it rained, water overflowed the gutters, and the nest washed away. If the nest survived the rain, the eggs fell out. If the eggs survived, the little chicks fell out. The sparrows cried, and so did our children. Their efforts to feed the chicks always failed, and the chicks died. The children buried them in the backyard in the row of wildlife and pet graves with stones on top.

So we sweep the nest and try to force the sparrows to build their nest somewhere else. But sparrows are stubborn. They try again and again. One year we changed the gutter. For a little while, the gutters were gone. It probably confused the sparrows, who moved elsewhere. After we installed new gutters, the sparrows stopped building their nest there. I was relieved.

Other birds also build their nests in the trees in our backyard. When a cat passes under their tree, they squawk and fly repeatedly over the nonchalant cat. We also see them chasing crows away.

The children find chicks under a tree. The cats haven't discovered them yet. Somehow they fall out of the nest prematurely. The children's efforts to feed the chicks and help them survive always fail. Finally, I call the Audubon Society for advice. They tell us to leave chicks that fall out of the nest alone, and to try to protect them from cats. "The chick will survive only if the mother manages to help it, and somehow takes it back up to the nest," they tell us.

As the chicks mature, they chirp loudly, demanding food. Sometimes I'm able to watch maturing chicks from a third-floor window. It's a pleasure to watch them grow. When it's time for the chicks to leave the nest, the parents stop feeding them, and the chicks chirp louder and louder, demanding food. After a little while, the chicks realize their parents won't feed them anymore, and they have to find their own food. Then the chirping stops, and the chicks leave the nest.

When I dig a vegetable patch in late spring to plant a vegetable garden, I find many earthworms in the soil. People from India say that soil containing earthworms is fertile. That must be true, because I manage to grow an abundant number of tomatoes, green peppers, cucumbers, eggplants, and a hot pepper in my little garden.

In the summer, when we have very hot days, earthworms crawl out of the ground, leaving behind corkscrew-shaped soil, and die in the heat. My efforts to pour water on them to help them survive fail. They die, leaving a flattened, dry tube behind. I have never understood why earth worms commit mass suicide. Despite their mass suicides, the number of earthworms in my soil does not seem to decrease.

In my vegetable garden, I find snails attached to some of the plants. The snail stays there for days. Sometimes I find a snail on a tomato. I pick that tomato and donate it to the snail.

Occasionally I find two snails stuck to each other. They stay like that for days, moving slowly. From the spot that they moved from, I see a white streak of sticky substance. I avoid stepping on them. One day they vanish.

When we moved into the house, there were no bunnies. Later on, I started to spot them. Now there are large numbers of them running around. I see baby bunnies, too. They're cute, but they eat vegetables, creating a big problem for those of us who grow vegetables in our yards. The discussion amongst neighbors about how to stop the bunnies from eating vegetables never stops. We don't have a solution yet.

Turkey in yard (photo by Michael Callaghan)

Turkeys are also a recent arrival. Last year I watched a turkey followed by five chicks crossing the road. The traffic stopped for them. I was really surprised. I had never seen wild turkeys in the city before. The group crossed the road slowly and went into another yard and disappeared.

This year, a single turkey crossed the road and walked into our backyard. Sharad promptly fed her sunflower seeds. She stayed there for a while, and then went away.

14

Then she started to show up every day for a meal. One day I watched her fly onto the top of the fence that separates our house from the next house. I wondered why she doesn't fly across the road.

Suddenly she stopped visiting. I don't know what happened to her. Did she get hit by a car? I don't think turkeys can survive in the city.

Now I hear coyotes are living in the city. I haven't seen one yet. I don't really want to see one. Human beings are encroaching on wildlife habitat. So wildlife is moving into our yards.

As summer approaches, and swimming season starts, lifeguards start to practice in the lake. Soon I see swimmers. Dog owners bring their dogs, and throw balls or frisbees into the lake for the dogs to fetch. I walk around on the pathway, and observe.

Children feed bread to the ducks. The ducks accept it hesitantly, floating in the water, and almost never step onto the land.

Then Canadian geese appear in the lake. I notice that the ducks avoid them. They stay away from the areas where geese are floating.

When children feed bread to the ducks, the geese come onto the beach, and fight for it, sometimes attacking children. One of the geese is so aggressive that someone hangs a sign around its neck, saying, "I bite."

Canadian geese show up in the spring and migrate in the winter. Then for some reason they start hanging around the whole winter. That causes problems for both ducks and people. Their droppings mess up the shore. People who live on the lakeshore start installing statues of owls to ward off the geese and keep them away from their yards.

Then one winter, it's so cold that the entire lake freezes. That winter, the flock of Canadian geese that had been living at the lake migrates. From that year onward, they start migrating again in winter. The balance of nature is restored.

At the end of the spring, when little children's games are done, adults organize their games. When they are short of players, they ask anyone on the playground to join. They accept any and all available players, including children, men and women. Players on the team are anywhere from 12 to 80 years old. I love to watch these games. The players are not interested in winning; they are playing for fun.

The summer ends, and the leaves start to change colors. Birds start to migrate. School and children's league games start. One day I see frost on the ground. I worry about the birds who haven't migrated yet. Soon the first snow showers paint the world white. If there's enough snow, children build snowmen and enjoy snowball fights. The playground turns white again.

The cycle of seasons starts again.

I wonder if a creature is watching me without my knowledge, and knows I am watching him or her.

Chapter 2
Salmon, moose, bald eagles, and other birds

Potter Marsh

A grand panoramic vista surrounds the Seward Highway as it exits Anchorage, Alaska. To the right is the Gulf of Alaska, which is part of the North Pacific Ocean and also part of a waterway called Turnagain Arm. Next to the ocean, alongside the highway, runs a scenic railroad track. To the left is Potter Marsh. The entire scene is framed by the green foliage-covered, snow-topped Chugach Mountain range.

Unlike other oceans, the Gulf of Alaska is like a lake: there are no waves. The water looks still, and shimmers in sunlight. I have seen pods of white Beluga whales there.

The water retreats at least half a mile when the tide is low, exposing mudflats that also line the shores. High tide flows back quickly as a wall of water, and is referred to as the bore tide. The mudflats are basically quicksand. Anyone who wanders onto them, ignoring the signs to keep off, can be sucked in and drowned.

Potter Marsh is man-made. When the Alaska Railroad was built, workers built an embankment to block Potter Creek, creating a wide ditch. Over time, nature turned the ditch into Potter Marsh.

The marsh is covered with 564 acres of tall grass. When Anchorage receives lots of rain, everything turns green. When the rain is scarce, brown patches develop. Sometimes there's water at the base of the grassy field. When the wind blows, ripples like ocean waves sweep across the grass, making a rustling sound. Part of the marsh is covered with bushes.

The surrounding mountains generate many rocky-bottomed streams or creeks of widths that vary from 2 to 19 feet, burbling through the marsh. Little ponds and puddles also dot the marsh.

An eight-foot-wide wooden boardwalk with wooden guard railings runs deep into the marsh, bending at right angles in two locations. Rotating binoculars are mounted on poles in multiple locations on the boardwalk so that visitors can view the marsh's wildlife.

We spend a couple of months in Anchorage every summer with our daughter and her family. When the weather is good, we try to visit Potter Marsh.

The marsh is a rest stop for many migrating birds.

Every time I visit, I hope to see swans, which are my favorite bird. I have seen both black and white swans in Potter Marsh. After a short rest, they fly north to nest and breed. When I visited the Arctic Circle, I saw them gracefully floating in ponds.

Swallows are always present in large numbers. They nest in birdhouses on wooden poles specifically built for them. Usually they are busy flying around. They sit on the boardwalk railing and are not afraid of people. I can be two feet from a swallow and the bird stays put.

Potter Marsh swallow

At least two or three pairs of Canadian Geese move into Potter Marsh for the summer. When I see a goose sitting in one spot day after day, I know she has laid eggs and is incubating them. When I don't see her at her usual spot, that means the eggs have hatched. I frantically search for the goslings. I don't always find them. But if I eventually see them, they are tiny, and can already swim. They are really cute. The mother is very protective. If she sees any flying bird, she collects them around herself. They grow rapidly. They have to grow strong in order to fly south.

Alaska bald eagle (photo by Andy Morffew via Wikimedia Commons)

The bald eagle is a huge bird. In Potter Marsh, a pair of bald eagles nest on the same tree every year. I always look for the nest. When I see one bald eagle sitting in the nest and another flying back and forth, I know the female eagle has laid eggs. Eventually I see — with binoculars, of course — little heads peeking out of the nest. Sometimes I see an eagle flying to the nest with a fish or a baby bird in its claws. Seeing a baby bird as a meal breaks my heart, even though I know that eaglets must eat. In six to eight weeks, the eaglets are gone. The nest is empty.

Numerous species of birds stop for a rest in the marsh. I have seen Arctic Terns. Some of the birds that can be seen there are northern pintails, canvasback ducks, red-necked phalaropes, horned and red-necked grebes, and northern harriers to name a few. After all these years, I still don't recognize them all.

Many varieties of ducks live in the marsh. If a game warden is present, he or she identifies them for us. I listen, but promptly forget their names. They are all beautiful. Sometimes we see ducklings in a row, following their mother.

Grass and water in the marsh attract moose. Moose belong to the deer family, and are huge animals. Twice I was lucky to see a mother and two calves. In Alaska, moose can be seen anywhere, including by the roadside. If upset, they will charge. I was once

Moose and babies (photo by Philip Shanahan)

charged by an adolescent moose while walking in a neighborhood. Safe on the boardwalk, I can watch a moose down in the marsh and don't have to worry about it charging me.

Muskrats and beavers also live in Potter Marsh. I have seen muskrats swimming in the narrow streams. I have not seen a beaver dam, but the marsh is huge, and a dam may be present somewhere out of sight.

A highlight of my summer in Alaska is the salmon run. The salmon arrive in pairs in late June, completing their epic journey.

Alaska salmon jumping (photo by U.S. Fish and Wildlife Service via Wikimedia Commons)

A salmon travels from the little pond or stream where it was hatched to a bigger stream, then to a river, and finally to the ocean. It lives there for five to seven years. Then a male and female pair travels upstream back to the pond or stream where they were hatched and spent the first year of their lives. Their keen sense of smell is their guide: they recognize their place of birth by following the water. The pair jumps over rocks and small waterfalls, fighting strong water currents and evading fishing humans, bears, and other obstacles.

When she reaches her birth stream or pond, the female picks a spot where she plans to lay her eggs. There she twirls and turns, thereby making the water cloudy. The female often turns pink before spawning. She lays her eggs under rocks by the shore, or under fallen tree branches —someplace protected. The male spreads sperm on the eggs. Having done all this, the parent fish die. The eggs incubate and hatch in two to three months. The salmon hatchlings then go through several developmental stages with names like alevin, fry, parr and smolt. As smolts — the last developmental stage before adulthood — the salmon reach the estuary, which is the point where a river connects to the ocean, and finally travel to the ocean. They live for five to seven years in the ocean, and then travel back to their birthplace to repeat the cycle.

I have been lucky to witness this miracle for several years. When I see salmon, it feels like I have seen God.

When the salmon run starts, bears visit. I have seen their paw prints in the mud by the stream, but I have never seen a bear in Potter Marsh. In June, the nights in Anchorage are only four hours long. I have no idea when the bears feed.

Homo sapiens also routinely visit the boardwalk. There are people like me who visit often. I have seen birders who come in groups, armed with binoculars and cameras. They shush anyone who talks. Sometimes children run and shout and irritate them. Periodically, a tourist bus parks, and many tourists emerge. The tour usually allows no more than half an hour for walking on the boardwalk. There are three port-a-potties in the parking lot. Some annoyed tourists spend their time standing in line and circling in place to look at the panoramic scenery. Others rush onto the boardwalk, trying to take in whatever they can see in the short time they have. People with cameras try to take pictures, then realize that the view is too vast to capture in a photograph. They pack away their cameras and try to memorize the scenery. The time is never sufficient to walk the full length of the boardwalk. They do the best they can and go back to the bus.

Occasionally I have seen a painter with an easel and paint brushes trying to capture the scenery. But the weather is unpredictable. Not many people try to paint the lovely scenery.

I consider myself lucky to be able to visit Potter Marsh every summer. I plan to keep doing it as long as I can.

Note: There are many varieties of salmon. This article provides only very basic information about the salmon life cycle

Chapter 3
Chico

We lived on a dead-end road. At the very end were undeveloped wooded lots. My daughters Veena, then ten years old, and Neena, six, frequently played there, along with other children living on the road.

One day, the group found a baby squirrel. When the children showed him some peanuts, he climbed up onto them and ate the nuts.

Veena and Neena brought the squirrel to our home to show it to us. It was cute. It had bright beady eyes and soft fur. It would climb onto a person's head and then run down, as though the person was a tree. It perched on Sharad's head, surveying the living room. The kids had already named him Chico.

Photo of Chico by Lalita Gandbhir

"Squirrels usually don't go near people," Sharad said. "But Chico is a baby. And he must have been hungry, so he accepted nuts from the kids."

For a short time, I watched the fun, staying away from him. Then a warning bell rang in my mind. The squirrel had pointy nails for climbing trees and sharp teeth for cracking nuts. I didn't want an armed warrior like that in my home.

"Now that's enough," I said. "You had your fun. Now take Chico and release him into those woods."

Immediately, eight angry eyes stared at me. Six were those of my family. Two belonged to the squirrel.

"I *knew* you would say that," Veena said.

"You're mean!" Neena cried. "We want him to live with us."

Sharad said, "Why do you hate poor innocent animals?"

"I don't want this rodent running around in my home," I said. "He'll scratch and bite. Squirrels carry rabies."

"Not true!" Veena said. "You said if a cat scratched me I could get cat scratch fever. And you said caterpillars are toxic, and that if I touched them I would get a skin rash. Nothing like that has ever happened to me."

But Sharad must have sensed I was right. "We'll keep him as an outdoor pet," he said. "You can feed him outside."

"But the other kids will take him," Veena said. "I found him."

"No, *I* did," said Neena.

"Never mind who found him," I said. "No mother would allow their kids to keep the squirrel as a pet."

Finally, we decided to release him for a few days and see what would happen.

A few kids were waiting outside for Chico. As soon as he was out of the house, a fight broke out over who had caught him and whose pet it was. Finally everyone, including a mother who had showed up after hearing the fight, agreed to Sharad's suggestion: "Chico will belong to all the kids that live on our road. He will live outside. Anyone can feed him."

For a short time, the idea worked. But Chico decided to adopt our family. He would wait on the maple tree in our yard. As soon as any man, woman, or child went out into the yard, he would run down the tree and climb up onto their shoulders or head and run down repeatedly.

Sharad said, "The kids found him just as he was supposed to learn to find his own food. Since the kids fed him, he didn't need to. Now he won't bother to find food for himself. He depends on us."

At first he didn't bite. But after a while, he started biting if he didn't get peanuts.

"He thinks people are walking trees with peanuts in their hands," I said to Sharad.

I was so scared that I stopped wearing skirts. I was afraid he would run up my leg and then dead-end. I started to throw peanuts into the yard to lure him away, before going outside. And I kept a box of nuts in the car, and would throw them before getting out.

Sharad and the kids continued feeding him peanuts when they were in the yard. Chico's presence outside our house and on their bodies didn't bother them.

The mailman came into our yard to deliver the mail. I told him to deliver it next door. When guests visited, I arranged for the kids to lure Chico away. Thankfully, he stayed away from the people who mowed our lawn. The noise must have scared him.

Then I got a phone call. A middle-aged friend of the family was planning to visit us. I knew the day and date, but not the time. This was a major issue. Like with a dog that bites, I had to control Chico. But how? How could I control a squirrel? I couldn't tie him up.

Then Chico bit Neena on the neck. She tried to hide the teeth marks, but I noticed. Worried about rabies, I called the pediatrician. He said there was no rabies in Massachusetts. That was a relief.

The night before guests were to visit, I had a dream.

A skinny middle-aged man and his plump wife, dressed in a sari, drove into our driveway. Chico immediately jumped on her and climbed up her leg.

She started to hop on one foot and then the other, screaming. Sharad and Veena came out and ran around her in circles, trying to catch Chico while he was on her foot. Sharad told me to spray water. "Where?!" I asked.

I woke up screaming.

The next day, I never took my eyes off the yard. The visit was uneventful.

When the guests left, I turned into Kalimata, the Goddess Parvati's warrior avatar, who destroys evil. Acting angry, I said, "Unless you promptly get rid of Chico, I'm going to buy poison and feed it to him."

"No!" Veena and Neena cried in unison. But even they knew that Chico was out of control.

Sharad said, "I don't want to kill him."

"I will," I said.

Sharad said, "We're going to be away for two weeks. I'll tell the neighbors not to feed Chico. He may forget us."

We went away for our two-week vacation.

When we returned, a squirrel sitting on the maple in our yard stared at us for two days.

Sharad had warned Veena and Neena not to feed Chico. "If you do, and he starts biting people again, I will have to kill him," he told them. The threat worked. They refrained from feeding him.

Eventually Chico disappeared from our life for good. Our lesson had been learned: Never feed a wild animal.

Chapter 4
A loon named Moony

Loon (photo by U.S. Fish and Wildlife Service via Wikimedia Commons)

We have a condominium in Singer Island, Florida that we love. When the kids were young, we used to like to escape there during school breaks, when the Northeast was snowy, with leafless trees and cold.

Singer Island is a barrier island — a strip of land with beach-lined ocean on one side, and a network of mangroves and a shallow intracoastal waterway on the other.

A row of high-rise buildings stands on the narrow piece of land between the two bodies of water. The warm weather and sandy soil support tropical vegetation, like coconut and other kinds of palm trees, as well as mango and orange trees, cacti, and tropical flowers. It reminds me of Goa, and in the winter it feels like heaven on earth.

In February of 1985, we flew to Florida with Raj, age seven, and Neena, fourteen. We stripped off our winter gear at the airport and, wearing short-sleeve shirts, had lunch, then drove to our condominium to deposit our luggage, and went back out into the sun for a walk. The warm breeze, the sound of waves, and the sunlight induced a kind of euphoria. We were happy.

We were walking along the shore of the intracoastal waterway. The tide was low, so the sand at the bottom was exposed. Near the coastline, little puddles of saltwater teeming with sea creatures were exposed. The children caught tiny fish in their cupped hands and released them. Sharad caught some little crabs, let them crawl on his arm, and then set them free. They saw a little seahorse swimming — a rare sighting. While they were playing, I busied myself looking at wildflowers. We were wandering aimlessly when all of sudden I heard Raj cry out, "A loon!"

I walked over to him, and saw a duck-like creature sitting in the middle of a little sandy island surrounded by mangroves, formed during low tide.

I did not know the difference between a duck and a loon, but I decided it was not the time to ask questions.

The loon didn't move, even as we moved closer. Raj, who was within two feet of it, said, "It's hurt."

Neena, who was close to him, said, "His skull is broken. I can see brain."

I knew then that our day would be spent tending to the loon.

Sharad pointed to a few vultures circling over our heads. "I suspect they're waiting for the loon to die."

I looked closely into the loon's beady eyes. I did not see pain. Instead, I thought I saw a sort of detachment. Unlike most wild animals, he didn't seem to care if we were close enough to touch him. It dawned on me that it might be because he was waiting to die.

Neena announced, "His name is Moony."

I wondered if she'd given him that name because he looked like he was not of this world.

"We have to take it to a vet," Raj said.

I said, "Let us look for a game warden."

Sharad waited by the loon to protect it from who knows what. I cursed our luck for finding the loon. The children and I searched for a game warden. A half hour later, we returned. We hadn't found one.

"Let's call an animal rescue league," Sharad suggested.

While everyone waited by the loon, I went back to the condominium and called the local animal rescue league. I talked to a volunteer about the loon. She asked a few questions, and promised that a knowledgeable person would call back.

Neena returned to the condominium to get water for the loon and Raj and herself.

After an hour, a woman called and said, "Our vans are busy picking up other animals. Can you please drive the loon to our shelter?" Then she instructed me on how to transport the wounded bird: "Get a box. Wear gloves and goggles. Gently pick up the loon and put him in a box. The loon will fight you. Bring the box to the shelter." She gave me directions. I wrote them down as best I could, but I knew we would be lost.

I had vinyl gloves and goggles. For a box, I knocked on our neighbor's door. When I told her why I wanted it, she said, "Do you think a loon with a fractured skull will live? Enjoy your vacation. Leave the loon alone."

I said, "I have a crazy husband and children."

She went back into her condominium and returned with a box. "Sorry to bother you," I said.

She laughed, "No bother," she said. "You are trying to save a life."

I went back with the box, gloves, and water bottle. The children were playing in the water. Sharad was waiting by the loon.

The children ran back to me. I handed Sharad the box, the gloves, and my goggles, and told him, "We have to drive the loon to the animal shelter. It's about 20 miles from here. Put the loon in the box. It will fight you."

When Sharad tried to pick the loon up, it suddenly came back to this world and fought him. Only someone like Sharad, who had skills from having handled wild chickens in India, could have done what he did. After a struggle, he managed to put the loon in the box and close it.

Off we went to the shelter. Soon we were out of the civilized world and driving on dirt roads with a lot of dust and no road signs. In other words, we were lost. Sharad cursed my directions. The water I had brought with me was gone. The children were thirsty but did not complain.

Eventually we found the shelter. It was surrounded by a tall wire fence, lined with tall trees. We opened the double doors and walked in with our box. The shelter had a roofed yard lined with wire cages, containing different animals and birds.

We were standing there wondering what to do when a tall man with a graying beard and dark blue eyes stepped out of the building, a serious expression on his face. He was wearing an apron. He approached us slowly. He reminded me of sages in old Sanskrit literature. A colorful bird was perched on his shoulder. "I'm Ron. What have we here?" he asked, and peeked into the box. As soon as he and the bird on his shoulder saw the loon, the bird screeched.

"Be quiet," Ron told the bird. "This bird was injured," he explained. "He's better now, but he can't fly, so he lives here and thinks he owns me. If I tend to other birds or animals, he gets jealous and screeches."

I hadn't known birds could be jealous.

The children looked at the bird lovingly.

A woman in an apron stepped out. "Jenny, you have a patient here — a loon," Ron said. "My wife Jenny is a vet," Ron told us.

"Hello," Jenny said. "Thank you for driving the loon here. Not many people would bother to drive here with an injured loon. Most wouldn't be able to pick it up and pack it in a box."

Unlike Ron, Jenny was smiling and talkative. "I have to take the loon to surgery, "she said.

"May I join you?" I asked.

"Yes, I love company," she told me.

The others scattered around the yard, looking at the animals in cages. "Feel free to look. Just don't touch them," said Jenny.

"They're wild animals, and they're injured," said Ron, and disappeared into the building.

In the surgery, Jenny put the box on the surgical table and bustled about collecting instruments, gauze, and other things she needed. She skillfully took the loon out of the box and put him in a cage. She examined him and cleaned the wound on his head, talking continuously the whole time.

"Loons migrate to Florida in winter," she said. "They dive deep into the water. Sometimes they dive too fast and deep, which causes a lung injury. Then they die. A vulture may have attacked and pecked him, and fractured his skull."

"Will it survive?" I asked.

For a moment she was serious. "The prognosis is guarded," she said, using medical jargon. "Let's hope it will. You can call and check how it's doing."

She bandaged the loon's wound and put it in a cage. I was sad for both the loon and for my children. I decided not to tell them about the prognosis.

"Thank you for helping animals," I said.

"I love my work," she replied.

When Jenny was done, I returned to the yard. Sharad, Raj, and Neena were busy looking at animals and birds in cages.

"Moony is taken care of," I said. "We can go."

"Will he be ok?" Raj asked.

I said, "Let us hope he will recover. When he's better, they will set him free."

Sharad went into the office to thank Ron. On his way out I watched him drop a few bills into the donation box.

When we left, the sun was setting.

I was impressed with Ron and Jenny's work and dedication. They were true animal lovers.

For a few days, I called to inquire about Moony. The volunteer who answered the phone said, "He is recovering."

After a few days, I stopped calling. When Neena or Raj asked me to call, I said, "I don't want to bother them. They are busy."

Eventually the children stopped asking.

I always wonder if Moony was wiser than we humans. Once he knew he was going to die, he did not make efforts to survive.

This article was published soon after we found the loon. Recently I tried to find the animal shelter we drove him to. I was not able to find it.

Chapter 5
Searching for turtles

On Florida's Atlantic coast beaches every year, an age-old ritual repeats itself. Leatherback, loggerhead, and green turtles nest in the sand. The most common, loggerheads, can weigh up to 250 lbs. The other kinds are less common, and even bigger.

Sea turtle laying eggs in ditch (photo by Dr. Dhimant Patel)

Turtle nesting season is from March through October. The turtles swim out of the ocean at night, and dig in the sand. In the ditch they've made, they lay soft-shell eggs, about the size of a tennis ball. After laying the eggs, they refill the ditch with sand, and return to the ocean.

The eggs incubate in the sand until they hatch, approximately two months later. The little hatchlings dig themselves out of the sand and scramble to the ocean. This usually happens at night, when the shiny ocean is their cue to head for the water.

Because the light of the ocean's horizon serves as the hatchlings' guide to the water, all the buildings near the beach are asked to keep any lights in the windows facing the ocean turned off. Lights on the beach itself are also turned off. If there is a light on the beach, the hatchlings go toward it, and can get lost and die.

The morning after the turtles have laid their eggs, volunteers come by and put sticks in the sand around the spot. Ropes are tied around the sticks to keep people away. The volunteers also keep an eye out for any hatchlings, and help them get to sea, because these turtles are endangered.

When we bought the condo in Florida and learned about the turtles visiting the beaches, we decided we had to see this natural wonder. That meant going to Florida between March and October, a timeframe we usually avoided because the weather is so hot. But to see this wonder, we decided to go in the summer when the kids would be on their summer vacation. So off we went in the middle of August, and had a taste of Florida heat. The sand on the beach burned the soles of our bare feet. But we didn't care, because we wanted to see the turtles.

At around 9 p.m. after dinner, we picked up our flashlights and went out to the beach right behind our building. From the top of the steps that lead from the building to the beach, I could see many figures running around on the beach in the dark, noisily laughing, shouting, and calling to each other. Someone from the 15th or 16th floor of an adjoining building was shining a powerful light from one end of the beach to the other. It looked like a searchlight. With all the noise and the roving searchlight, I wondered if *I* would visit the beach to lay eggs if I were a turtle.

I had other reservations, too. It was so dark we could barely see each other's faces. I wondered what would happen when we got down to the beach. The steps leading from all the buildings looked similar. How would we recognize our own building's steps in the dark? And how would we find the children if we lost sight of them, which seemed like a strong possibility? And what if the children went into the water? How would we keep an eye on them?

Seeing me hesitate at the top of the steps, Sharad said, "What are you waiting for? Let's go."

"It's so dark," I said. "What if the children get lost?"

I was about to say more, but he wasn't interested. "You dragged us here all the way from Massachusetts to see turtles," he said, "and now you have doubts? You don't have to come if you don't want to, but we are going."

The children were already down on the beach. He went after them, took their hands, and started to walk. My options were closed. I went down, too, and told them to stay with us. Fourteen-year-old Neena said she would be all right and would take care of Raj. "No," I said firmly. "You two stay with us."

As I expected, my instructions were a waste of time. We walked together for a short time. Then, from one end of the beach, somebody yelled, "Turtle! Turtle!" The entire crowd ran over. Neena also ran, holding Rajesh's hand. I couldn't keep up with them, so they were gone.

When we reached the spot where the crowd had collected, a woman told me it was a wooden board that someone had mistaken for a turtle. I was disappointed. And now the kids had disappeared.

Luckily Sharad was still with me. We turned to looking for the children. I saw two kids playing in the water. I yelled at them, telling them to get out of the water. When we went closer, I realized they weren't mine. Those kids didn't seem to mind, though. They obediently stepped out of water and sprinted away.

Finally we found our children. Luckily, they were together. By now a few teenagers had decided that fooling the crowd was fun. So they yelled "Turtle!" from the other end of the beach, and the whole crowd ran there.

By now, I had stepped on shells and stones, and injured my feet. Neena and Raj had already rushed to the spot where the teenagers were yelling.

The people shining the searchlight must have seen the crowd move, so now they were shining the searchlight onto the crowd. When we reached the spot, Neena said, "There is no turtle. Those kids played a trick."

I had become convinced the turtles would not show up that night. Sharad agreed. We dragged the kids back with us. They thought what was going on the beach was fun. We could hear someone yelling "Turtle! Turtle!" from the other end.

The next day, a neighbor told us we needed to go to the beach later, after the crowds had gone home. He had gone and had seen a turtle. He showed us a picture as proof.

For two nights, I tried to wake everyone up around 2 a.m. to go see the turtles, but everybody refused to get up. I didn't want to go alone. We tried going again after dinner, but no turtles appeared. Finally we gave up, and decided to be happy with the pictures our neighbors showed us.

That was long ago. I've still never seen a turtle laying eggs on the beach.

Chapter 6
Bat Encounter

Bat woodcut from Popular Science Monthly Magazine, January 1875

We had just moved from a cozy little colonial house into a large Victorian. The house was old. The floorboards creaked, the heating system was noisy, the third floor had dark rooms with a sloping roof, and the basement was old, dark, and smelled of mildew. One of the bathrooms was old, with a bathtub on four legs.

We moved in December. The days were short, and that year, it rained all the time. The girls, who disliked both the house and the move, started saying the house was haunted. They wouldn't go to the third floor by themselves.

One evening, after the girls were asleep, Sharad and I were in the living room, sorting out papers, when I thought I noticed something moving in the hallway near the staircase to the third floor. I ignored it. But it happened again and again. Finally I said, "This house really *is* haunted. Something is moving in the hallway."

"You're imagining things," Sharad said. Then I saw it again.

I couldn't ignore it this time. I went into the hallway.

Something was flying — or more like zooming — in the narrow space, no more than six inches wide, between the staircase bannisters, which bent acutely and went up to the second, and then the third floor. It raced up and down with lightning speed.

"A bat," said Sharad.

"Yes," I said. "The house is haunted, so it must have bats. Now the atmosphere is complete."

My knowledge of bats was limited. All I knew was that they lived in caves and in haunted houses, and carried rabies.

"How can it fly in the narrow space between the staircase banisters?" I asked.

"Because bats have sonar," Sharad explained. I had no clue what sonar was.

While we were talking, the bat had now disappeared.

"Our windows are closed," I said. "How did the bat come into the house?"

"She must have flown in through the chimney or eves," Sharad said. "Because of her sense of sonar, she can fly up and down fast. Let's open the windows. She might fly out."

We opened the windows and screens. In five minutes, the house was freezing. The girls woke up, wondering what was going on. Then they saw the bat, which had now reappeared. It flew around a few times, then disappeared again. The girls were fascinated.

After half an hour, we closed the windows, hoping the bat had flown away.

But it soon reappeared again.

The girls went to bed. I was not happy to have a bat flying freely around the house.

I looked up bats in our encyclopedia. I learned that they're not birds, but mammals, like mice. The bat's wings are stretched skin. Through their mouths and noses, they make high-pitched sounds, which we humans can't hear. They can hear the sounds they make rebounding or echoing. With the help of this echolocation sense, they can hunt at night. Apparently dolphins have the same sense. Their eyesight is poor.

"What would a bat hunt in our house?" I wondered.

We searched the house for the bat, but we didn't find it. Sharad said that if he could shut the bat into a room, he could then catch it with a towel and set it free outside. He used to catch bats in his home in India. But those homes were single-story, so it was easy to corner a bat.

We slept with all the bedroom doors open.

Worried that the bat might bite one of us in our sleep, I slept lightly.

In the middle of the night, I woke up. In the dim light of the night light, I could see a shape flying near the ceiling. I shook Sharad. He started chasing the bat with a towel he had handy. But before I could close the door, the bat flew out of the room. Sharad chased her until she disappeared. Again we couldn't find her.

The next day, we opened the windows for two hours. I was worried that with the windows open, the bat might invite its relatives and friends into our home.

Sharad chased the bat whenever we saw it, but in vain. This went on for four days. Then the bat vanished. We decided it had flown out.

After a week, I went into one of the third-floor rooms. Someone had inadvertently closed the door. Inside, in one corner, I found a tiny mouse-like creature, dead on the floor. I screamed, and everyone rushed upstairs.

"Someone closed the door," Sharad said. "Locked in this room, she starved to death."

The girls cried. "She must have been thirsty," he said. Then I cried.

We buried her in the backyard.

Sharad had someone cover the fireplace chimney with a screen so bats wouldn't fly in anymore.

I will never forget how fast the bat could zoom up and down.

Chapter 7
Florida wildlife

Spoonbill stork and white ibises (photo by Rekha Keluskar)

We started spending whole winters at our Singer Island, Florida condominium in 2013. Soon afterwards, the grandchildren began joining us there during their winter school vacations.

On Singer Island, wildlife is everywhere. We regularly see turkey vultures and pelicans in the trees around us. We also see pelicans diving into the waterway to catch fish. In a parking lot, we once encountered a duck with a red, bead-like crown on its head. And we've seen

Egret

41

lovely egrets feasting on geckos in a garden.

The geckos are everywhere. Our grandchildren watch them, fascinated.

We soon discovered that there are many parks nearby, located on conservation land set aside for public enjoyment and recreation. We started frequenting these parks, which we and the grandchildren love, in addition to the beach.

All the parks have winding trails that crisscross Florida vegetation, and bring us into unexpected encounters with the area's wildlife.

* * * *

Florida Gopher Tortoise (photo by Tom Friedel via Wikimedia Commons)

One beautiful park near our condominium is officially named Frenchman's Reserve. But our grandchildren named it "Tortoise Park," because so many tortoises live there. Tortoises look like turtles, but unlike turtles, they live on the land. As we walk the trails, we often run into one slowly crossing our path. Nothing seems to rush the tortoise. Once we found one walking slowly around in the parking lot. Afraid it would get run over, we stood around it, wondering how to move it to a safer area. I wanted to pick it up and put it on the trail, but I was afraid, thinking it might bite. Soon another car arrived. The lady that emerged from it solved the problem. She picked the tortoise up and moved it to the trail. I was impressed.

Dogs aren't allowed in the park. Once, someone ignoring the notice was walking a dog. When the dog came across a tortoise, it went crazy, struggling to get to it and pulling on its leash. The owners wisely decided to leave.

42

The park has a little pond, with no boating or fishing allowed. Occasionally we've seen a sea cow (or "manatee") floating there. Manatees are gentle, and move slowly through the water. Egrets or blue herons often stand by the shore, fishing. They stay stock-still until they see a fish, then they suddenly dive into the water, pick it up, and gulp it down

Many snakes live in the park, too. Once, while walking on the trail, Sharad stepped on a small pile of leaves and suddenly jumped two feet into the air. As we watched, a colorful snake slithered out from under the leaves. After that, the children started calling it "Snake and Tortoise Park."

* * * *

At the north end of Singer Island is the John D. MacArthur Beach State Park. The kids call it "Kayak Park." A sandy path from the parking lot leads to a building with a gift shop, a museum, and an auditorium. Visitors can rent a kayak there.

Blue Heron (photo by Vaishali Shukla)

A boardwalk is built out over a large expanse of the shallow Intracoastal Waterway. Visitors can cross it and go to the beach. The Intracoastal also serves as an estuary.

When the tide is high, we rent a kayak. When it's low, the sand at the bottom of the waterway is exposed, and a kayak can get stuck on it. I've seen people who tried to kayak at low tide walking in the Intracoastal, dragging their kayaks behind them, because the water wasn't deep enough for the boats to float.

While kayaking, many birds can be seen fishing in the Intracoastal. I've seen herons, pelicans, terns, egrets, sandpipers, osprey and gulls. Loons are also on the scene. They float gracefully, then suddenly disappear into the water, only to reappear far away, floating again.

Sometimes manatees can also be seen floating in the water.

On the mangroves that line the shore, I've seen tree crabs. They match the trees perfectly, and are hard to spot. If they sense any slight movement nearby, they disappear.

Florida tree crab (photo by U.S. Fish and Wildlife Service via Wikimedia Commons)

* * * *

Wakodahatchee Wetland is in Delray beach. The kids call it "Bird Park." It has 50 acres of wetlands, with bushes, grass, other vegetation, and a boardwalk that winds through it all. It's approximately three-fourths of a mile, with benches and covered areas in the middle. The wetland supports numerous species of birds, crocodiles, iguanas, rabbits, frogs, and more. The city pours millions of gallons of treated wastewater into the wetland, where it is purified and can be reused.

Storks in tree at "Bird Park"

The children named this park Bird Park because of its population of storks that nest there and raise chicks. One of the trees with nests is very close to the boardwalk. Visitors can see the chicks with their open beaks, and the parents feeding them. The parents fly again and again to fetch food for the babies. The flying birds are graceful, and the sight is fascinating. After the chicks grow up and leave the nest, the cycle starts all over again.

There are also many alligators in this wetland. Once we were lucky enough to see approximately ten alligator hatchlings. They were in constant motion in the water while their huge alligator mother lay still nearby.

Another time, I saw three or four snakes wiggling through the water. They moved fast and disappeared under the boardwalks.

I have also seen different kinds of ducks there. They are too numerous to recount.

Whenever we visit Bird Park, we always see one or two iguanas. Some are big, while others are small and colorful. When we first visited Florida in the '80s

Iguanas (photo by Neela Inamdar)

we never saw iguanas. They started appearing sometime later. Now they are everywhere.

Wider view of tree with storks

＊ ＊ ＊ ＊

Grassy Waters Preserve is a 23-square-mile preserve that supplies water to the Palm Beaches, and is part of the northern Everglades. It's a watery landscape, with grass, bushes and other vegetation. From a scenic boardwalk, visitors can walk deep into the preserve, and feel a sense of total isolation from the world.

Wild peacock (photo by Rekha Keluskar)

In the preserve, we've seen turtles, herons, egrets, belted kingfishers, and alligators. On the blackboard outside the preserve's office, people write the names of birds they have seen. There are many more than I mentioned above.

Night heron (photo by Rajashree Palkar)

These are just some of Florida's many parks. The wildlife there is different from that seen in cold climates. I am still learning about it.

Chapter 8
Safari

In 2013, five of us — four adults and one ten-year-old — went to Tanzania for a Safari.

Over five days, we visited Tarangire National Park, Serengeti Park, Ngorongoro Crater and Lake Manyara in that order. The two parks are similar. We stayed in different hotels each night — three nights in regular hotels, and two nights in tent hotels. In this piece, rather than chronologically recounting each day, I describe some of the highlights of our trip.

We woke up early each morning, had breakfast, and started driving right away, because the animals are usually out in the morning and easiest to spot then. We brought box lunches with us, or ate lunch at hotels along the way. We had to be back at our hotel by 6 p.m. every evening, because there was a curfew in the parks after that.

Our tour guide was also our driver. The original Toyota Land Cruiser we rode in had been modified for safaris. The back was cut off, and another truck-like extension with a seat had been added. It had thick tires that could travel over the rough roads with rocks, steep slopes, ditches, and mud. The top was cut off so that travelers could stand up and look around. Rubber tubing had been added to the outside of the vehicle, so if it went through deep puddles, water would stay out. The engine was also protected from water with rubber tubing.

The park's roads were unpaved, made of red soil, and had many ditches and rocks. It was wintertime, which is a dry season. Due to the lack of rain, the road was dusty. The route was unmarked.

As we approached Tarangire Park, the driver instructed us not to get out of the jeep. "Wild animals are used to the jeep," he said. "But they are not used to seeing humans outside of it. If they see a human, they will assume the person is a threat, and will kill them."

"Some tourists," he warned us, "ignore the guides and get out and are killed. Just because you don't see any animals around, don't assume there aren't any. The grass is tall, and lions and leopards can hide in it. If they see a person, they can run really fast and kill them. Animals in the park do not eat humans — they kill them."

I wondered what we were supposed to do about a bathroom, but didn't ask.

The park was covered with tall grass, which was brown because of the winter dry season. Between expanses of grass were bushes and occasional trees. (This grassy wilderness is called savanna. It is not like forests or jungles, covered with trees.)

In the park, we saw groups (called "crèches") of graceful impalas grazing. Far away, we could see wildebeest herds.

We drew close to a lake, and saw a huge female elephant walking toward it. Behind her came another smaller female elephant, and a couple of little elephants (or calves). We stopped to watch as they went into the water. The two little elephants and one of the older females started to play, spraying each other with water. The two little ones were jumping on each other and collapsing into the water. The big female elephant came back out, rubbed herself against a tree that was only about ten feet from our jeep, then picked up a piece of wood with her trunk, and started scrubbing herself with it. When she was done, she blew dust on herself. The guide explained that the dust protects elephants from the sun. Totally ignoring us, she went back into the water.

The other three elephants continued to play. The medium-sized female elephant was most likely the two little ones' older sister. She apparently didn't need to get out of the water to scrub herself, as she wasn't a teenager yet, and didn't need to groom herself. I was trying to guess what the mother elephant was thinking. I decided that just like a human mother who has finished swimming and wants to go home, she was done, but the younger ones refused to leave. Just like kids — they couldn't resist a pool of water.

The guide finally decided to move on. He told us the elephants might continue in the water for hours.

After a mile, we encountered a herd of zebras. They were on both sides of the jeep. Ignoring the vehicle, they were crossing the road. There were many foals in the herd, who stuck close by their mothers. One of the foals was lying on the grass. We stopped and watched. Within a few minutes, it struggled and stood up. Its legs were wobbly. The zebra mother was licking the baby. Slowly the foal straightened out and started to suckle. I realized we had just missed the birth by a few minutes. The foal's curious older cousins and aunts circled the pair, watching them. Other zebras seemed nonchalant, and focused on grazing. Very slowly, our driver continued on.

After half a mile we encountered a large troop of baboons with red bottoms. The driver had to stop, because they were on the road, and there were little ones crossing with the group. One male baboon was on the road picking through elephant dung. He kept picking something out of the dung and eating it. The guide explained that 60% of what an elephant eats doesn't get digested, so it gets excreted. The dung contains berries and nuts, which are foods that interest baboons. Another male baboon showed up. He tried to pick food out of the same lump of dung, but the first male objected. They fought, and the second male retreated and went to a different lump. The first male acted like he owned all the lumps. He went over and started to fight. They both stood up on their hind legs and showed their teeth, dancing around, growling. A few younger monkeys collected around them, and watched with great interest, the same way human kids would watch a fight. Finally, the second male gave up and ran away.

All of a sudden, all the monkeys acted as if they had received a warning message. I didn't hear any kind of alert myself, but the infants in the group abruptly jumped onto their mothers' backs and hung on for dear life. The whole troop ran away, jumping into the grass and up into the trees or bushes if they could find one. The male monkey, who had been carefully picking through the dung, momentarily hesitated, then finally gave up his treasure and joined the others.

Then we drove to a river. It was shallow, burbling through many rocks. A group of mongoose were rushing around among the rocks. While I was watching the mongoose, two lionesses crossed the road right in front of our jeep, then crossed the river. They found a clearing by the river and sprawled comfortably. The guide said that they must have just had a meal and were now resting. He also guessed that the monkeys, and possibly also the zebras, must have run away because they smelled the lionesses. We admired them for a long time. Then we crossed a rickety bridge and went around a small hill. There we noticed a lioness sitting on a rock. She looked sad and appeared to be crying. I was shocked to see this powerful animal crying pathetically. The driver said that the lioness was most likely lost. The two lionesses we had seen crossing the river must be her companions. She was probably looking for them. She was big, and we could see that she was ready to give birth. She needed help. She was lost at the wrong time. We watched her for a while. I wanted to tell her where her friends were. Then she got up and went down the hill towards the river. The driver said that she must have sensed where her friends were and was on her way to rejoin them. I was happy that she had found them.

We continued on and ran into a troop of baboons. They were on one side of the road, and a crèche of impalas was on the other. A male monkey was standing in the middle of the road on his hind legs, showing its teeth, growling, and shaking his arms in the air as though he was fighting. I was wondering who he was fighting with. Then we saw a young impala stuck in the bushes near the monkey troop. It looked scared. It was watching the male baboon, who was obviously threatening or teasing the young impala. The guide said that the baboon was most likely an adolescent and acting up. Baboons generally don't bother foals. As we watched, the young impala jumped high, and with lightning speed, crossed the road and ran away. The baboon looked shocked, and kept standing where he was. Then he joined the rest of the troop. Suddenly, both the baboon troop and the impala crèche started to run. The guide said that the lionesses we had seen must have moved, and the impalas and baboons must have received a signal that they were approaching.

With predators nearby, prey animals have to be in a state of constant fear and alert.

After a little distance, we ran into some more baboons. As with the previous group, a large male was sitting in the middle of the road, digging through elephant dung. Two infants approached him and started to bother him. They jumped on him and climbed up onto his shoulder. He pushed them away. But they came back and continued to bother him. He tolerated their mischief for a short while, then slapped them both. They ran away screeching.

A little further on we drove close to a river. A line of elephants was approaching the river from the other side. Just as I had seen in pictures, the elephant calves were in the middle. The elephants entered the river and started to bathe, splashing water on themselves with their trunks. The calves started to play in the water. The guide explained that elephants are generally safe in the jungle. Lions don't bother them. A crocodile could pull a baby elephant into the water and kill it, but they don't do it, because the mother elephant would drag them out of the water and jump on them. If a crocodile bothers an elephant calf, it doesn't survive. The only true enemy elephants have are humans who kill them for ivory.

We watched a herd of zebras running on both sides of the road. They ran fast, the little ones struggling to keep up. In a short time they were gone. They were obviously running away from a predator.

Then we ran into a herd of male elephants. The guide called them a "bachelor group." He said that these elephants were old. The female elephant who rules the herd throws older male elephants out. These old elephants live together and form a small group. They have no shortage of food, but they are lonely. This is the law of the jungle. Female elephants, no matter how old, stay with the herd; they aren't kicked out like male elephants. I don't understand the logic. There is plenty of food, so the old elephants aren't a burden.

Next, we saw two hippos who were fighting. They were butting heads. A hippo calf was hiding behind a female hippo, who was fighting a male (or "bull") hippo. The guide said that hippo bulls frequently kill calves, so the mother was protecting the calf. I was upset. Why would a male hippo kill the calf?

Then we watched another elephant herd. One of the baby elephants in

the group was limping. The guide said that poachers frequently set up traps. The baby must have gotten its leg caught in a trap, and become injured.

We stopped to look at a female leopard at the top of a tree. Two cubs were stranded at the bottom. One of the cubs started to run away. The guide said that if a cub runs away from its mother, it won't survive alone.

At one point, we noticed a group of hyenas all running in one direction, and saw vultures circling overhead. The guide said that an animal must be dead nearby. Hyenas don't hunt. They steal from other animals who hunt.

For a couple of nights, we stayed in a tent camp. There were many hyenas around the camp. We could hear them all night. Once, we saw a cruel-looking hyena whose face was completely covered with blood.

One day we ran into a pride of lions. There were lions everywhere — lions, lionesses, and lion cubs of different ages. They surrounded our jeep. I saw what looked like the king of the jungle: a really handsome lion, who must be the ruler of the pride. The entire pride must have been traveling somewhere, because it kept on moving. Hypnotized, we watched. After the whole pride had gone, three little cubs showed up, looking scared. Somehow they had not kept up with the pride, and were now lost.

Another jeep full of women was following us, watching the lions. The women in the group were so emotional that they were crying. The guide said that the sight of majestic lions often makes people cry.

The guide drove us to a hippo lake. According to the guide, hippos don't go walking around in the afternoon, so it was safe to stand nearby. Even though it was called a lake, it looked more like a U-shaped river. Many hippos were floating in the water. Hippos cover themselves with their own dung to protect themselves from strong sunlight. Standing close to the river, I started to feel nauseated from the stench, so I moved away and stood under a tree. I thought it was safe, because the guide had said hippos don't get out of the water at noon.

Hippos are territorial. A hippo will kill anyone in its way. As I stood there, a hippo waddled out of one arm of the water and headed towards me. I ran back to the group of people. The hippo quietly went back into the water on the other side, walking right over the spot where I had been standing. The guide said it was a lucky escape. Hippos have very weak eyesight; it didn't see me. So it quietly walked into the water on the opposite side. The incident shook everybody, including two other groups of tourists standing there. We got into our jeeps and drove away.

Hippos, elephants, and lions don't bother crocodiles. And crocodiles don't bother hippos, elephants or lions. That's the law of the jungle.

In many rivers, we saw crocodiles. When the wildebeests run through the water, crocodiles feast on them. Most crocodiles we looked at hardly moved.

Lions hide near watering holes. When animals come to drink, they hunt them. We were near a watering hole, watching animals drink. Some zebras were drinking when three or four lionesses sprinted out of nowhere and jumped on one. The zebra fell to the ground. A few adolescent lions jumped on it and killed the zebra, though it fought valiantly. Then the whole pride of lions arrived to feed. There was a hierarchy to their feeding, too. The big lion, who had not hunted, pushed the others, except for little cubs, away, and started to eat. But after that, there was a feeding frenzy. All the lions were trying to get their share and fighting. Soon some hyenas arrived, and circled the lions. The lions tried to drive them away. The hyenas retreated, and tried again and again.

The zebra herd collected under a tree and started to bray. The guide said that they were warning other animals that lions were near the watering hole. I thought they were mourning and crying. One zebra jumped in place non-stop.

We noticed some dik-diks trying to hide behind a bush. It was a rare sighting. These are tiny deer (a kind of small antelope). Their eyes were slanted, jet black, and so lovely that I understood why in Sanskrit literature a beautiful woman's eyes are said to be like a doe's eyes.

The guide showed us the outcropping where they filmed the live-action version of *The Lion King* at Serengeti Park. That's when I learned that the film was really filmed where it was supposed to take place.

Dung beetle

At a lunch stop, we saw a dung beetle. According to the guide, a dung beetle is an important creature that contributes to cleaning up the forest and fertilizing the soil. It collects huge balls of dung and buries them. It builds a nest in those dung balls.

Our next stop was Ngorongoro Crater.

If anybody has just one day to see Africa, I would recommend this crater.

It was once a volcano. The volcano calmed down, but the ditch containing lava remained. The ditch is a hundred square miles.

It was early morning when we reached the edge of the crater. As we looked down, the rising sun was shining on the lake in the crater. Many streams flow from the lake and crisscross the crater. The water shimmered in the sunlight. The rest of the crater was covered with grass that was mostly green with some dry spots. Masai tribe huts were scattered in the crater. They were arranged in circles. Each group of huts was surrounded by a fence made of tree branches. The mountains around the crater were covered with dense vegetation. The crater itself had very few bushes.

Driving down into the crater, we ran into a group of Masai children. They were dancing by the side of the road. When we asked the guide

why lions don't bother Masai children, he said that they cover themselves with the juice of vegetation* that keeps lions away, and that they carry spears.

Kids as young as ten were guarding herds of 20 cows. Tourists weren't allowed to step outside the jeep for fear of their being killed, but young Masai kids were wandering around freely. It was a striking contrast.

The grass was short enough that we could see wildebeests and buffalo from very close, and they were totally visible. A herd of buffalo was grazing in one area. They look similar to the water buffalo in India, except that they're tall and overall much bigger. Their faces look fierce, and they always look like they're ready to attack at any moment. They graze in groups. Four or five buffalo are always standing at the edge of the grazing herd, scanning for enemies.

Buffalo herd

The calves are always in the middle. Buffalo are the only animal that dare to attack elephants. All other animals who graze live peacefully, ignoring each other.

Wildebeests are skinny. They have hair on their neck. They migrate in June or July. We were in the crater at the wrong time, so we didn't see the migration. But I did see many wildebeests running together in a line. I had to satisfy myself with that sight.

Wildebeest

When we got to the lake, wildebeest were running along its edge. Around the lake, water buffalo herds were grazing. Warthogs were wandering around between the buffalo and the wildebeests. Vultures were soaring up above. A group of flamingos (called a "flamboyance") was standing still in the lake, their pink wings shining in the sunlight. Egrets were fishing in a stream. Masai huts dotted the scene.

I felt like I was in prehistoric times. The scene is permanently etched on my mind.

We noticed a king of the jungle. He was crouching in the grass as if he was going to hunt. He was most likely planning to attack a wildebeest. The guide said that lions that live in a pride don't usually hunt, but that this lion was alone because he was kicked out. One lion rules a pride. When the ruling lion is old, another stronger lion fights with him and drives him away. So the old lion has to hunt to feed himself.[*]

We also saw some hippos floating in the lake.

Our last stop was Lake Manyara, which was surrounded by rainforest. It had so many colorful birds that I lost track of their names. Flamingos and many of the other animals we had seen before were there, too. There were also blue monkeys.

Flamingos

An electrified fence protected the hotels we stayed at. We weren't allowed into the surrounding garden; we had to stay indoors. The tent hotels we stayed at were modern, with tarp walls and a roof like a house, and nice attached bathrooms with brick walls and a door that opened into the tent. One of the tent bathrooms had no roof. Monkeys would sit on the top of the bathroom wall. Again, we were not allowed to step out of the tent. The whole camp was guarded by a Masai man carrying a spear, a guard carrying a gun, and another man with a flashlight. I learned that animals are afraid of flashlights and fire. All night, the guards walked around the camp flashing lights. The campfire also burned all night. We had to have a guard walk us to the tent where they served food. In both the tent camps and regular hotels, we could hear animals howling all night. I actually saw an elephant walk right by our tent camp. Somehow I wasn't scared.

Safari ant

Outside one of the tent camps, the ten-year-old we were traveling with stepped onto a row of ants. They climbed up on him, and went into his pants. Anyone who went to help him suffered the same fate. The ants went on biting for 40 minutes. The bites were very painful. I learned what "ants in your pants" means.

Throughout the safari, I watched the wild animals' behavior closely. I realized that human and animal behavior is very similar. We are related. But there is one distinct difference. Animals don't manipulate or lie. They take from nature what they need to survive and no more.

Once upon a time, the whole world was like the parks we visited.

When the safari was over, and we landed in a Zanzibar resort, I had culture shock. I wondered what the land the resort was built on had once been like.

These parks are special because they have existed since time immemorial.

Nine years after the trip, I still dream that I am in Africa in those parks.

The details of Masai tribe life and lion prides are beyond the scope of this article.

Chapter 9
Elephant back safari

In 2013, my husband, my son, and I went to Victoria Falls in Zimbabwe. At the time, in addition to the spectacular falls, an elephant sanctuary offered a safari by elephant-back.[*] We had just done a similar safari in Tanzania, where instead of riding an elephant, we rode in a jeep.

Elephant back rides weren't a novelty to me. I had seen people on elephants since childhood. In India, rich people had wedding processions featuring the bride and groom riding an elephant, and in religious processions, religious idols are mounted on elephants' backs. Historically, elephants were also used like horses during wars. But riding an elephant through a wild landscape surrounded by animals like lions, crocodiles, wild elephants, hyenas, and wild buffaloes was something else.

I had learned during our Tanzanian safari that animals in the African wilderness don't bother elephants. The only animal foolhardy enough to attack an elephant is the buffalo. Sometimes a buffalo tries to hurt an elephant with its horns. But that's rare.

So theoretically, a person riding an elephant is safe. But if a domesticated elephant were to encounter a wild elephant, the situation could be dangerous. And what if one of us were to fall off the elephant? Wild animals and crocodiles would be close by.

But it was a unique experience. We had already risked a safari. We decided to risk an elephant ride.

A van picked us up at our hotel and brought us to the elephant lodge. It was made of wood logs, and was built over a small river, surrounded by jungle. From the balcony we could see hippos, crocodiles, and ducks in the water. Beautiful colorful birds were flying around, and I could see other wild animals nearby. Inside the lodge there was a theater with tiered seating. A screen was set up for showing a film.

After all the vans had arrived, everyone was invited into the theater. First we had to sign a consent form.

Then there was a brief talk. The guide explained how the sanctuary acquires elephants. "We don't catch elephants," he explained. "Most of them are injured for one reason or another. When a dominant male elephant in a herd gets old, a younger bull elephant kicks him out and takes over as the dominant male. He tries to kill any young elephant calves fathered by the former lead male. Mothers try to save their little ones, but often they get injured. If we find a young injured elephant, we care for it. The calf drinks three gallons of milk a day. These young elephants become used to caretakers, and can be easily domesticated. Sometimes poachers set traps, which catch an elephant's leg. These elephants limp, and often find themselves alone and in need of help. We care for them and treat their wounds. Though wild, they can eventually be domesticated. If an elephant is trapped in a fire and injured, we save them."

Then he explained how to get onto an elephant by climbing a wooden platform, then climbing from the platform to the elephant's saddle. Each elephant would have three riders. The rider in the front would be the caretaker assigned to look after that particular elephant, and would guide the elephant through the wilderness. In addition to the caretaker, two additional people would ride each elephant. Any single travelers would have to find a partner.

We waited in the lounge balcony for the elephants to arrive.

When they got there, the elephants lined up one behind the other. The first elephant stopped at the platform. Like the guide had described, each elephant was being ridden by its caretaker, who sat in front. The saddle had a wooden back and stirrups, with a peg in the middle. To demonstrate how to climb onto the elephant, the guide climbed onto the platform. He held onto the peg on the elephant's saddle, then he climbed aboard the elephant and put his feet into the stirrups. Then the second person climbed on behind him. It was important to lift one's foot off the platform quickly, before the elephant moved.

We were standing in the line. I carefully watched all the guests ahead of me climb onto their elephants. They all did it successfully, but they were all taller than me. Two guides were standing by, helping guests. I was hoping for a small elephant. Instead, when it was our turn, a huge elephant walked up to the platform. I struggled, but climbed on behind my husband, and held on to him for dear life.

After the whole group had mounted, the line started to move. Three men walked in the front and at the end of the line with guns. The landscape was just like the one we had seen in Tanzania: partially dried tall grass, with scattered bushes. During our ride, we saw many hyenas. Four ostriches were also nearby, as were many impalas. Buffalo and wildebeest herds were at a distance, and we saw a few giraffes. We didn't see any wild elephants. There may have been lions hiding in the grass, but we didn't see any. The animals that we saw completely ignored our procession.

Most of the ride was uneventful. While walking, our elephant casually broke the branches off trees that were in his way. That was how he cleared our path, rather than walking around the trees. The guide explained that elephants often casually uproot trees and break branches.

The only time I was scared was when we crossed a creek that was shallow, but deep in the middle. The elephant had to step down a slope and then climb back up to reach level ground. The caretaker clung to the elephant's neck. We were pushed forward and backward. There were alligators in the stream. If one of us were to fall off, we would have made a good meal for them. But we managed to stay aboard.

Learning about the elephants we were riding, and their relationships, was interesting. Three mother elephants were walking with their calves. One baby elephant stopped to nurse. The entire line stopped. Then the baby elephant got distracted by a tree, and we started to move again.

The caretaker explained that when a female elephant has a calf, other female elephants get jealous. They fight with the mother, and the calf can get hurt. So the sanctuary separates mothers and calves from other female elephants. Male adolescent elephants also fight, so the sanctuary tries to separate adolescent males from each other.

After 40 minutes, we returned to the sanctuary. The elephants lined up by the platform and we climbed down onto it, which was easier than getting on.

Next, we were going to feed the elephants, which was their reward for taking us for a ride. But before feeding them, the hyenas had to be fed. If hyenas smell pellets, they come into the sanctuary. The hyenas are fed so that they stay out. After the hyenas had been taken care of, the elephants lined up behind a fence. The guide showed us how to feed them: he picked up some pellets in his cupped hands, and put his hands in the elephant's mouth. Very few people had the courage to put their hands in an elephant's mouth like the guide did. Most just threw the pellets into the elephants' mouths. Apparently the elephants knew they would get pellets after the walk, so they willingly allowed us to ride them.

After we had fed the elephants, we were invited back into the theater to watch a film of our ride. Everyone watched, mesmerized.

The DVD of our ride was for sale. Everyone bought a copy. The guide requested that we visit the gift shop and buy souvenirs, because the sanctuary desperately needs funds to pay caretakers, maintain the sanctuary, and feed the elephants.

I was really impressed with the dedicated people working there, and with the sanctuary.

I also learned that elephants, like humans, have emotions. They can be jealous, and fight. I loved the calves who walked with their mothers. I will never forget the unique experience.

In the time since we went on the safari, a general understanding has developed that elephant riding is problematic for elephants, and elephant riding is no longer available at Victoria Falls. At the time we went, we were unaware that it could be detrimental to the animals.

Chapter 10
Glow worms and mini penguins

Glow worms in Ruakuri Cave, Waitomo, New Zealand (photo by Joe Ross via Wikimedia Commons)

In New Zealand, we visited glow worm caves. They are located on New Zealand native lands, and are managed by New Zealand natives.

We had to wait in one line to buy tickets, then in another to go into the caves. When we entered the cave, the line became single file, because the passageway was so narrow.

The cave was dark, but we could still see. As the line slowly moved forward, the light got fainter and fainter, until we were in the pitch dark. Terrified, I held on to my husband's hand until we reached a river. There, helpers in a dim ray of light helped us into a boat. I realized we were floating down a river in a cave. Many worms were glowing like stars on the ceiling and walls of the cave. The sight was so beautiful that I was hypnotized. A moment earlier I had been terrified, but as we floated down the river, my fear vanished, and I wished we could float on and on.

Again it was pitch dark. Slowly the boat floated into an area that had dim light. We stepped off the boat. The path progressively had more and more light. Finally we stepped into daylight. I felt like I was waking from a dream.

Later on, I learned that if the worms are exposed to light, their glow disappears. Moisture from the river that flows in the cave helps them survive.

The subterranean river and the glow worms in the cave are the most amazing natural wonder I have seen.

* * * *

In Australia, we went to a beach one evening before dusk to see miniature penguins. Wooden boards were arranged in step-up fashion on wooden poles, like bleachers. There were approximately ten tiers. We settled down on one of the wooden boards. In front of us was a 20-foot-wide sandy beach. All we could see was beach and ocean. Behind the bleachers was a wide expanse of four-to-five-foot-tall bushes.

Australian mini penguins (photo via Wikimedia Commons)

The bleachers were very crowded with restless and noisy people. Kids were running around on the beach. Guards walking on the beach asked everyone to sit down and be quiet, because noise scares penguins. But as soon as the guards left, people stood up, blocking the view of the people in the back. They resumed talking loudly.

When the sun was almost ready to set, a group of penguins swam to the beach. Suddenly the crowd went silent, and everybody sat down, including the kids.

The penguins were about fifteen inches tall and blue-gray. They swam from the ocean and stood up on the beach, looking around. Then the group gathered together, facing each other. They seemed to consult each other like a group of friends discussing an important matter. They then went back into the water. Next they swam back to the beach, and again consulted each other, as if trying to make a decision, before again going back in the water.

This happened a few times. Then all of a sudden they formed a line and waddled, one behind the other, and disappeared in the little one-foot-wide dirt and sand paths in the bushes that lined the shore. More and more penguin groups arrived and repeated the same actions, then disappeared into the bushes. The crowd watched silently. After half an hour to 45 minutes of this, we were instructed to walk on the fenced boardwalk that crisscrossed the bushes. The little penguins were waddling along the paths through the bushes and disappearing into their nests. I could see the entrance to their nests (or "clutches"). It was covered with bushes. I tried to bend over and look inside, but I couldn't see anything. (We were not allowed on penguins' pathways.) The little penguin families were in their nests. Just like humans returning home from a day at work, adult penguins had come home after a day of feeding in the ocean.

We walked on the boardwalks until it was time to leave. We couldn't get enough of the magical world of mini penguins.

Chapter 11
My friends the hornets

We went away for two months, leaving our house locked. When we returned, I went into the backyard and noticed a nest straddling two motion-sensitive lights attached to the back of the house. Insects that looked like wasps were flying in and out.

Cautiously, I stepped closer. The nest was artistic. It consisted of identical layers of overlapping, semicircular structures made of a wood-like material in various shades of black, with a white lining. Insects were flying in and out of gaps between the layers. Slowly I moved even closer. A couple of insects circled my face and flew away.

We consulted a pest control company. They sent a technician who said it was a hornets' nest.

Curious, I googled to learn some basic information about hornets.

Hornets belong to the wasp family. They eat caterpillars, spiders, aphids, and mosquitos. They also pollinate plants. They sting only if they or their nest are threatened. If injured, a hornet sends a signal. Other hornets promptly respond and attack the offending human or animal. One hornet can sting again and again, and their sting is poisonous, causing a painful bump and sometimes a severe allergic reaction.

Each nest usually has two or three queens whose only job is to lay eggs. Then there are male and female hornets. Females do all the work. They collect food, feed the hatched larvae, the queen, and the males. The males do nothing other than chase females. Females are out of the nest, busy collecting food all day. In the winter, the queens leave the nest and bury themselves in the dirt. The other hornets die. When summer comes, the queens start another nest.

I was most surprised to learn that hornets recognize faces. When I went close to their nest for the first time, I was in the backyard. When I was in the backyard or porch, occasionally a couple of hornets circled my face and went away. I walked by their nest often and they didn't bother me.

I did not know how they communicated to all the other hornets that I was their friend. I decided that all of them knew me.

I soon noticed that I could sit on a chair in the evening in the backyard free of mosquitoes biting. The hornets were hunting mosquitoes. That was wonderful. Our backyard was mosquito-free.

I had many friends living in the nest in my backyard. I liked them.

Occasionally, one or two hornets continued to circle my face and went away. For a couple of months, they left us alone. I was happy to have them.

I did not wish to destroy their nest. But soon we had to leave and go to Florida. If the nest had not been constructed on top of the electric lights, we could have left it alone, and the hornets would have naturally died when the weather changed. We were waiting for a freeze. Finally, freezing weather did arrive, and lasted two days, but the hornets were very much alive, and continued to zoom in and out of their nest.

I continued refusing to destroy it.

Unfortunately, its location, on the motion sensor lights, was a real problem. And the nest was getting heavier. My husband was worried the bulbs might collapse.

"We have no choice," he said. "We have to call pest control."

"I don't want to kill my friends," I protested.

"Their life is almost over anyway," he pointed out. "If we wait much longer, there could be a short circuit, and our house will burn."

"Besides," he added, "the pest control man said the queens are most likely already gone."

I cried, but eventually consented, and we called pest control.

The technician said not all the hornets would be killed. "Anywhere from 2 to 300 will be out of the nest when I destroy it," he said.

I shed tears, but the nest was gone.

For two days, I avoided the backyard. On the third day, I walked down to the back porch and started to do my exercises. Two hornets circled my face and went away. They did not bite me.

Sad, I invited them to build a nest on a tree branch next year and said goodbye.

This story first appeared in Marathi, in Ekopa, *November 2021 online audio issue as 'Gandhilmaashyaanchyaa sangateet' (In the company of hornets), as written by Dr. Lalita Gandbhir and read by Dr. Veena Shah. The Marathi original can be read and heard by signing in at https://www.aickum.org and clicking on the November 2021 issue of* Ekopa.

Chapter 12
A spider named Valya

Photo via Wikimedia Commons

The covered front porch of our Victorian house had two round poles on each side of the front steps. The poles were approximately six inches apart. A pair of adjacent Rhododendron bushes in the yard abutted them. Spiders loved to weave spiderwebs between the poles, and between the poles and the rhododendron bushes.

Every morning in the spring, summer, and fall, I had to sweep the front porch. I couldn't stand the dead leaves, the dry fallen petals from my hanging plants, the dirt that the children's shoes tracked in, and the spiderwebs on the poles.

I didn't like sweeping the webs. I felt guilty for ruining the spiders' hard work. I knew that spiders build webs to catch prey to eat. Like

72

everyone, a spider needs to eat. But I didn't understand why the spiders kept building their webs between the poles when I swept them away every other day. Why couldn't they move elsewhere? The spiders were stubborn. But I was stubborn, too. I didn't want the front entrance of my home decorated with webs. So the cycle of the spiders building their webs and me sweeping them away continued.

One morning, I saw a spiderweb and a spider that made me pause. The spider was tiny, with a red dot on its back. But the little spider had long legs that bent multiple times. The web the spider had built was beautiful. Instead of the usual one-dimensional web, this spider's web was multidimensional, connecting the poles and the rhododendron bush. Dew drops on the spiderweb were shining like diamonds in the early morning sunlight. I stopped. I decided to leave this spider with the red dot on its back and his web alone. The spider sitting in the center of his web looked like he was meditating. I stood there for at least five minutes, watching him. He totally ignored me.

I named the spider Valya, after a character in the Sanskrit epic Mahabharat, even though the original Valya character was human.

When Sharad got up, I showed him the spiderweb and the spider. "His name is Valya," I told him. Sharad liked the web and Valya. "Leave Valya alone," he said. "Don't sweep him. I need to catch a fly," he added.

"A fly? What for?" I asked.

He was already trying to catch one.

"To feed your Valya," he said.

"You are crazy," I said. "A spider can catch his own meal." I left him on the front porch, trying to catch a fly, and returned to the kitchen.

A little later, Sharad came into the kitchen. "I couldn't find a fly," he said. "So I found a big black ant to feed him."

Raj, who was eating breakfast, asked, "Feed who?"

I said, "Valya the spider."

Raj stopped eating. "What? A spider?"

Rather than answer his questions, I said, "Come with me."

I dragged him to the front porch, and showed him Valya.

"Your father is killing ants and feeding them to this spider," I told him.

"I like the spider," Raj said.

We noticed a dead black ant in the spiderweb. The spider hadn't moved.

"It's not fair to the ants," Raj said.

He finished his breakfast and went upstairs to argue with his father.

I didn't pay any attention to the argument.

That evening, the ant had disappeared.

Sharad fed Valya every day, and every day, Raj argued with him. This went on for a few days. Then there was a huge storm, and itsy-bitsy Valya and his web were washed out.

We lost Valya with the red dot forever. Many spiders weaved their webs on our porch poles again, but the cute spider with the red dot never reappeared.

After that, I stopped sweeping the spiderwebs. I left them alone, and nobody noticed them.

Part Two

Pets

Chapter 13
An animal lover's childhood

Water buffalo in India (photo via Wikimedia Commons)

My husband, Sharad, was born and lived in a city, Kolhapur, Maharashtra, for the early years of his life. They lived in a *vada*, a multifamily dwelling, with a small yard that they shared with many families. The kinds of pets Sharad could get in Kolhapur were limited. He had a dog, a cat, and chickens.

When Sharad was 11 years old, the family moved to a small town named Kankavali, Maharashtra. The population was most likely five- or six-thousand. The town was still preindustrial. Their house was built of soft red stone bricks, and the walls were covered with mortar. They had dirt floors. The roof was made of clay tiles. There was no electric power, no drainage system, and no town water. The family had to draw water from the well. At night they used lanterns or oil lamps. They also had an outhouse.

But the family's home had a large yard. Sharad was totally comfortable there, and was set free to roam as he pleased and keep as many animals as he wanted. He didn't care if his mother approved or not. He kept them if he could.

School in Kankavali was not the best, and Sharad was not interested in learning. His ambition was to own a horse and cart, or many animals — like water buffalo and chickens — and somehow earn a living. Many local farmers' children dropped out of school after the first few grades. Their illiterate parents wanted them to learn to read, write, add, and subtract, then stay home to help with the farm work. Sharad envied them.

His mother consented to buy the water buffalo and chickens that her beloved eldest son wanted, because she had many children, and thought that a water buffalo and chickens would provide plenty of milk and eggs for them.

But caring for a water buffalo is a major chore. The buffalo had to be driven to pastures outside of the town to graze. And someone had to spend the day there watching her, because there were wild animals in the forest nearby. The alternative was to feed her in the barn with hay bought at market.

The water buffalo also had to either be driven to the river to be washed, or get washed by well. Someone also had to clean her barn. And of course, someone had to milk her twice a day.

The yard had to be fenced, because water buffalo attract hunting animals, like tigers, at night. And periodically a water buffalo has to have a calf in order to keep producing milk.

Chickens need less care. They wander around in the yard and feed on grain scattered there. At night they have to be collected together and locked in a secure room reserved for animals. Most of the time, the chickens walked by themselves into the room reserved for them. Sharad would make an "aaa aaa aaa" sound, and the chickens would flock into the room. Once collected together, they were grouped and covered with wicker baskets. If they had been allowed to roam free at night, they would have attracted foxes, wolves, and other wild animals. Usually they laid eggs in the room reserved for them. The yard was messy because of chicken droppings. Someone had to constantly sweep it.

It's easy to find inexpensive help in rural India. So the family hired Gangaram, a boy of 15 to help. He stayed with the family to help take care of the animals, and did other chores. Sharad treated him like a playmate.

Running wild, Sharad learned the art of catching scorpions. A scorpion's sting is very painful. He also tried his hand at catching snakes, then stopped, because he realized how dangerous a snake bite can be. In India, snake bites are often poisonous, and can be fatal. But he and our children catch snakes in the U.S.

One day, running around the town, Sharad noticed a cute little baby goat (or "kid") on the road. The goat must have wandered away from his mother. Sharad decided that he would keep the goat as another pet, so he carried it home. He offered it a dish of milk, then tied it to the bed in the bedroom. The baby goat seemed happy. But after sundown, it started to bleat for its mother.

Sharad's mother heard the bleating, found the goat, and was exasperated. "He is just a baby, and he is hungry," she said. "He needs his mother's milk." It was nighttime, and the roads in Kankkavali were pitch dark, so they had to wait until morning. After sunrise, Gangaram and Sharad went searching for the owner. When they found him, the owner didn't realize that it was Sharad who had picked up the goat and carried him off in the first place. So he thanked them profusely.

Sharad's mother, who was often alone because her husband traveled for business, had difficulty controlling her son. She lectured him, and told him not to bring home stray animals. She added spankings* to drive the point home. But her son couldn't control himself. He continued to bring home puppies and kittens.

Sharad also had a parrot who lived in a cage. He fed him fruits, hot peppers, and other vegetables. One day, someone opened the door to the cage, and the parrot flew away. Sharad chased after him, climbing trees, but he couldn't catch the bird. It was gone, and Sharad was sad.

When Sharad was 13, his father was transferred to Karwar. The family had to move, and the buffalo was sold.

In Karwar, Sharad had only a dog (a fox terrier named Namya), and a cat named Mani. Mani was female and had kittens. One of her kittens died by falling off the roof. Mani cried all day for her lost kitten.

The move to Karwar marked the end of Sharad's childhood. But his love for animals persists. He still picks up stray dogs from the road, and our children do, too. His grandson tries to save half-dead voles, and baby bunnies hunted by cats.

The tradition continues.

Spanking was a common form of punishment in India at the time and even now.

Chapter 14
Tomya the dog

When I was growing up in Pune, in a bungalow with extended family, Tommy (or "Tomya") was our dog. He was a small brown mutt with sad eyes that made people, especially children, pity him and try to pat him. Sometimes Tomya welcomed their attention. But other times, without any other expression of his annoyance, he would bite them and run away.

As a puppy, Tomya had belonged to an English family that planned to return to England from India. They needed a family to adopt him. My older cousin Vasant liked the cute puppy, and brought him home. My Aunt Honibai and my grandfather, Kaka,

Photo of a dog that looks just like Tomya (by photographer Jamie Street via Unsplash

loved the puppy, and decided to keep him. Even though Tomya was in fact a totally Indian dog, our family pronounced him to be English, and gave him the English name Tommy[*] (or the Indian version, "Tomya.") For a long time, I told my friends that Tomya was English, because a British family had owned him. They believed me.

Kaka and Honibai were Tomya's primary caretakers.

When Tomya was a puppy, he fell from the stairs and got a head wound, which bled profusely, and required seven stitches. According to Honibai, the fall had given him a brain injury, which affected his temperament, causing him to bite people. Honibai's implication was that it wasn't Tomya's fault that he bit people.

Only Honibai and Kaka could feed Tomya. His food, which was leftovers from what we ate, was served in an English (meaning aluminum) dish. To feed him, Kaka tied him to a balcony railing. A loud announcement would be made: "Tomya is eating!" because if anyone got too close while he was eating, Tomya would bite them. Only Kaka or Honibai could safely walk within range of Tomya . Someone had to watch out for young children. Once he had finished his food, he would curl up and sleep.

In the morning, which was a busy time of day in the household, Kaka or Honibai would tie Tomya to a balcony railing. He would alternately whine, bark, or howl, disturbing any children who were trying to study, and any family trying to listen to the radio.

Finally, sick of the noise, someone would lock all the doors leading out of the second floor, and, after loudly announcing, "Tomya is free! Do not open the doors!" would set Tomya loose. Tomya would stay where he was until someone inevitably forgot the announcement and opened a door. Then Tomya would shoot out the door and out of the yard. No one could catch him. He would wait on the road, and when anyone left the house, he would chase them to wherever they were going.

My Uncle Gangakaka was usually the first person out of the house. He had to catch a bus to get to work. Tomya would chase him to the bus stop, and then chase the bus, before eventually coming home, looking for a second person to chase. That person was often me.

I walked to school every morning, and every morning, Tomya would chase me. I tried to hide from him in temples along the way, hoping he would go back home. Sometimes he did, but I ended up late to school, and would be punished.

At that time, a few people in the area had water buffalo herds, which they would walk to pastures outside Pune. Sometimes I would walk back towards home in the middle of a herd, hoping Tomya would go back. Tomya had once chased a water buffalo, who had kicked him and dropped dung on him. He lay on the roadside, injured and covered in buffalo dung, until a neighbor noticed him and informed the family. Kaka wrapped him in a blanket and carried him home. He washed Tomya and fed him mutton soup. After a week, Tomya had recovered, but the incident had left him mortally afraid of water buffalo. I could get rid of him by walking among the buffalo, who were usually docile. But I was endangering myself.

If I could not lose Tomya, and he made it to school, I had to walk back home. He would follow me. By that time he would be hungry, and would go into the house, where Honibai would tie him up. I would return to school, having already missed a class or two.

When family members travelled, they hired a tonga (a horse-drawn carriage) to go to the train station with their luggage. Then Tomya chased the tonga to the station. Following the family members, he managed to sneak past the ticket collector onto the platform and tried to jump onto the train. But the carriage entrance was too high for him. When the train started moving, he chased the train past the platform as far as he could.

Other travelers were impressed. "What a loving, loyal dog!" they said.

Tomya was unpredictable. If someone started to pet him, he would welcome it. He would jump on them, wagging his tail. But sometimes he would suddenly change his mind and bite the person.

The family endlessly discussed how he chose his victims. According to Honibai, he bit people who looked cross. That was not true. He would be sleeping in a corner, suddenly wake up, bite a person reading the newspaper, and take off. Tomya bit me and my cousins many times. His bite was superficial, like a scratch. Honibai, who was always partial to Tomya, blamed the children. She would rub a cotton swab soaked in iodine on the wound, and ask, "Did you tease Tomya?" Never mind that I had done nothing more than walk into the room when Tomya decided to bite me.

I accused her of loving the dog more than she loved me. She said, "You can talk. Tomya is a poor dumb animal."

Over time he bit my friends and other cousins' friends, the mailman, guests, deliverymen, and the businessmen who visited my father, Baba. People started to stand on the road and yell, "Is the dog tied up?" before they would come in. Outside of our yard they were safe; Tomya only bit people when they came through the front gate into the front yard.

Tomya also chased men who rode bikes on the road in front of our bungalow, entangling himself in the back wheel. And he would chase cars and tongas. Finally a horse kicked him, so he stopped chasing tongas. Occasionally a cyclist complained. Honibai had the nerve to blame the cyclists. "Our dog chases people who don't dress properly," she would say. Or "Our dog knows when people are mad at him." Most of the cyclists were young college students. They could not argue with an older woman. They didn't argue, and went away. Her irrational arguments astonished my father.

When Tomya bit a child, the parents showed up, and a fight started. My father, Baba, promptly left the home from a side door.

Honibai again stepped forward. As usual, she blamed the child.

Faced with a furious man, she had the ultimate weapon. "I will poison and kill the dog," she said.

In our nonviolent Hindu culture, killing a dog was unacceptable. The angry parent suddenly changed their tune. "No. No. Please don't kill the dog; Keep him tied up, or send him to a farm."

Baba hoped Tomya would get himself killed. But like a cat, Tomya had nine lives. He survived being kicked by a horse and a water buffalo. Then, when he was chasing a car, a front wheel hit him, at least according to witnesses. He was unconscious for a while. But after a few days, he was himself again.

In Pune, the river flooded during heavy monsoon rains. People went to a bridge called Lakadi Pul** to watch the wild river. Some adventurous souls jumped into the gushing water. My cousins had gone to see the flooding river. Tomya had followed them. One of them said, "Tomya will be able to swim in the river." The other said, "No, he will drown." So they made a bet and threw Tomya into the river. He vanished.

Honibai and Kaka were furious. Baba and my Aunt Akka were relieved.

Tomya was missing for three days. Then he showed up.

After one peaceful month, he resumed his biting and chasing routine.

As usual, the family could not decide how to deal with Tomya.

Akka really disliked him. Honibai and Kaka loved him. Baba would have tolerated him if Tomya had not bitten so many people. Rabies was prevalent in Pune then, but no one worried about it.

Finally, Baba decided to send him away. Tomya was sent off on a truck. The truck dropped him in a remote village. After a couple of months, he returned. He stayed for a few months, and restarted his biting routine.

Finally, Baba had him tied up in a sack, and asked a truck driver to set him free in a remote village.

This time Tomya did not return.

Honibai was sad. Sometimes I still dream that I am walking to school and Tomya is chasing me.

* In India, pets were often given English names.

Chapter 15
Anjell and Shadow

Because my young daughter loved animals, we adopted a cat.

His name was Simon, and he was an orange male tabby cat. We didn't know about the concept of neutering cats when we adopted him. Maybe that's why he was so wild. He fought with other male cats, and likely also skunks, because he would sometimes come home covered in skunk spray. My husband would wash him with tomato juice and hose him off. Then one day a car hit him and we found him dead by the side of the road.

The second cat we adopted went outside one day and didn't come back. We never found him.

Our third cat, named Kalu (which means "black" in Hindi), was found dead in the neighbors' yard. When we called the vet, he said that sometimes cats eat mice that have eaten mouse poison. The poison kills the cat.

Upset, I decided not to adopt any more cats. The anguish over losing the cats was painful, especially for our little girl. She didn't understand the concept of death. But she understood that the cat was gone forever. Every day, she asked for another cat.

Photo of cat resembling Anjell (by Alexey Komarov via Wikimedia Commons)

Finally we succumbed, and adopted a female cat named Anjell. We got her as a little kitten. She was all white except for a little black spot on her chin. She was playful and cute like all kittens. We kept her in the house, and didn't let her out until she had been spayed. The veterinarian had said that spayed cats are docile. Anjell wasn't

85

docile after she her surgery, but she survived.

Anjell loved my daughter and followed her to school, which was only one block from our house. She would sit on my daughter's first floor classroom windowsill, attracting the children's attention and disturbing the class. Sometimes she would go into the school and into my daughter's classroom, disrupting lessons. Someone had to put her out.

After the school called to complain, we started locking her in the house when my daughter was heading off to school. But she still managed to sneak out whenever the door opened. Finally she came to understand that she wasn't welcome in the school. I'm not sure a cat has enough logical thinking to figure out why we were locking her in, but she stopped going into the school. From then on, we set her free in the mornings.

Our second daughter was soon old enough to demand her own cat. So we adopted another kitten, named Shadow, who was black and white. She was cute and playful like Anjell. At first, Anjell didn't like Shadow. But soon she accepted her, and they lived together happily.

We were going to get Shadow spayed when she was the right age. But there must have been an error in calculating her age, because before we could schedule the surgery, we discovered she

Photo of a cat resembling Shadow (via Wikimedia Commons)

was going to have kittens. I wasn't happy, but the girls were thrilled. Soon our basement was home to a litter of kittens.

We now had five cats. The three kittens were really cute and playful. Shadow was protective of them for a while. But when they got older, she shoved them away. The girls were shocked and surprised. "Does she not love them anymore?" they asked me. I told them that animals are different. They aren't attached to their children for life the way humans are to their children.

The girls were happy to have five cats, but I was not. I decided to give the three kittens away.

A sign posted outside the house saying, "Free kittens," brought no takers. I had to find homes for them. So I decided to take them to a fair. We put them in a cage and set the cage on a table and waited at the fair entrance.

We didn't have a permit to set up a booth, but nobody objected. A huge crowd of children collected around us. Every child wanted a kitten. Finally we found three parents willing to take them, and the kittens had new homes.

Soon at our home a doorbell problem started. We would hear the doorbell ringing. When we opened the door, we saw nobody there. But Anjell would come zooming in. Soon I figured out she had learned how to climb up on the railing by the steps outside the door and ring the doorbell with her paw. "Smart cat," everybody said. But she would ring the doorbell at all hours. So we started keeping her locked up after she had her dinner around 7 p.m.

If Anjell wanted to play when our daughter was studying, she would sit on her open book and not let her read.

Shadow was a hunter. She killed mice and brought them home, leaving little presents around the house. If we didn't find it promptly, a terrible stench announced a dead mouse in the house. The girls didn't mind, and would hunt for the dead mouse. I hated to pick it up. So the girls did it, and buried it in the backyard, putting a little stone on the top of the graves. After a while, our backyard had a whole row of graves.

Then our son was born. By then we had had those cats for almost eight years. They were part of our family. Our son had severe allergies. He had been admitted to the hospital three times by the time he was two. The third time he was admitted, the doctors advised me to create an allergy-free house. I had to get rid of the drapes and carpet, and we stopped bringing nuts into the house.

What to do about the cats was a real dilemma. At first we tried to keep them in the basement. But it turned out to be impossible to get them to stay there. We had to get rid of them. Finally a colleague of my husband, who lived on a farm, agreed to take them in. The girls cried, but we had to send the cats away.

We drove them to their new home and returned without the cats. A month later, my husband received a call. A gentleman on the phone said that there were two cats in his garage. He had looked at their tags and called us. My husband called his colleague, who went and picked the cats up.

The next week, we visited the cats at the farm, but they walked away. I think they may have been angry with us. Eventually they adjusted and stayed there. To date, I am not sure whether giving away the cats helped our son.

The girls were angry and still are. The trauma lingers.

Chapter 16
Big Red and Henry

My daughters had cats. But they weren't satisfied. They also wanted a dog. Our older daughter Veena even pretended to walk a dog twice a day to show that she could take responsibility for one. But still, I refused to yield.

Photo of a dog resembling Big Red (via Wikimedia Commons)

One day, my husband went to Cape Cod for business by himself and returned with a dog, an Irish setter. The dog was handsome, a deep russet color. He followed my husband into the house and looked around by himself. The girls were thrilled. They named him Big Red. The cats didn't appreciate the intruder. They puffed themselves up, backed into a corner, and growled. Totally ignoring the cats, Big Red drank the water that Sharad offered, went upstairs, and settled himself in the girls' room. While Sharad went to buy dog food and a leash, the girls sat by him and petted him. I watched. Big Red was relaxed.

Sharad returned, fed Big Red, then leashed him. Big Red didn't resist. The girls and Sharad took him for a walk. On the road, people stopped to admire him. Neighbors asked if he was our new dog. The dog heeled perfectly while walking. If one of the girls lingered, he waited for her. Our town had strict leash laws, so Sharad couldn't set him free. All of them had to walk together.

Then they went to a park where Sharad was allowed to let Big Red run free. On the playground, the dog stayed by our younger daughter Neena's side. Wherever she went, he did too. When she fell, he sprinted over to Sharad, barking. Sharad realized something was wrong and went to check on Neena, who needed comforting for a few minutes, then started to play again.

I actually liked Big Red. He was housebroken and well behaved. After the girls went to bed, he slept in their room on a blanket.

I asked Sharad where he found the dog. He said that he'd found it running along the side of the highway. Sharad had been worried that a car might hit it. He looked like a nice dog, not a stray. The dog had a tag around his neck. So Sharad pulled over and asked the dog to come to the car. The dog ran to him, and when Sharad opened the back door, the dog jumped in. Sharad stopped at the local police station and informed them before bringing Big Red home.

"What are we going to do with him?" I asked.

He said, "We'll keep him. He's a really nice, well-trained dog."

I asked, "Who is going to walk him? What happens when the girls are at school and we're at work?"

He said, "We'll leave him in the house and see what happens."

We did just that. The next day, instead of picking up the girls from after school care immediately after work, I rushed home to walk Big Red first. He was waiting by the door. I walked him, then brought him back home, then picked up the girls and brought them home. He welcomed them by wagging his tail and licking their faces. He didn't jump on them. I looked through the house. It was clean. He had waited for me.

I wondered what we would do when we had to go away for a couple of weeks. But I decided not to worry about it. I liked Big Red.

The dog settled into our home. Both cats accepted him and ignored him. The girls loved him. He was big, but so well behaved that our ten-year-old could walk him in the neighborhood by herself.

We forgot that Sharad had notified the police on the Cape about the dog, and that they had our phone number. Two weeks later, we received a phone call. A gentleman was looking for his lost Irish setter. The owner had located us.

We were heartbroken, but the dog had to go back to his home. The owner showed up a couple days later. Big Red walked to him slowly and jumped in his car. When they left, the girls were crying. I thought Big Red looked sad, too. He turned to look back at the girls. But he went. We missed him. Even our neighbors were sad. But we had to let him go.

I told Sharad, "I will take a dog like Big Red anytime."

Not too long after Big Red had gone, Sharad showed up with another unexpected visitor, a dapple dachshund.

He was hotdog-shaped, like any other dachshund, but had lovely silver spots on his fur. He had a pathetic expression in his eyes that made everyone pity and love him. He was meek, wagged his tail, and let anyone pet him. The girls, who adored any and all animals, loved him right away, and hugged him. He was small, so they could pick him up and hold him on their laps. They decided to name him Henry because they thought he looked royal.

Photo of a dog resembling Henry (via Wikimedia Commons)

Irritated, I asked Sharad, "Did you find him on the road?"

"I bought him," Sharad answered. "I was in the pet shop, and he was for sale. He used to be a show dog. But after he lost his baby teeth, one of his big teeth grew in crooked, so he couldn't be a show dog anymore. He used to be valued at two-thousand dollars, but because of the crooked tooth, his value dropped to $50."

"There's only one problem," Sharad said. "Because he was a show dog, he's spent his whole life in a kennel. He's not yet housebroken."

Upset, I said, "That's a major problem. Who's going to housebreak him? We're both working."

Sharad said, "Next week I'm working from home. I'll housebreak him."

I said, "My knowledge about dogs is minimal, but I know that you can't housebreak a puppy in a week. Can you housebreak a grown dog that quickly?"

He said, "That's *my* problem."

Aware that the children were watching anxiously, I stopped arguing.

We still had a leash and dog food from the Big Red episode.

Sharad fed him and offered him water. He didn't eat, but he did drink some water. Then the girls and Sharad walked him. He was easy to walk, but scared of people and children that wanted to pet him. He was also scared of other animals, and anything that moved, including a falling leaf. Sharad guessed that because he had spent 18 months of his life in a kennel, he was insecure, and not exposed to the world. He was like a scared puppy.

When our next door neighbor John heard about our predicament, he suggested that we walk Henry with his dog Spot, so that Henry could learn from Spot how to behave when out for a walk.

When they walked together, Sharad tried to get Henry to smell the spot where Spot had peed. This went on for a couple of days. Henry didn't learn. He preferred carpet, hardwood floor, and kitchen linoleum. After a week, Sharad was exasperated and accepted defeat. So did John.

The girls cried, but Sharad had to take Henry back to the pet shop. The shop owner said, "I *told* you that Henry would be difficult to housebreak, and that you should buy a puppy instead." Sharad had to give him a hundred dollars to take Henry back.

We learned a hard lesson. It isn't possible to housebreak a kennel dog. At least, it's not something that we were able to do.

Chapter 17
Lucifer

One day, a transparent glass bowl appeared on our dining room table. A few fish about the size of my little finger were calmly swimming in the bowl. They were silver and red, and they looked pretty shining in the sunlight. Since I didn't have to worry that they would jump on anyone or bark or make a mess, I decided to overlook the fact that fourteen-year-old Neena had imported them into our home without my permission.

In the days that followed, I noticed that their numbers were slowly declining.

Neena bought more from Woolworths. I wondered why the fish were dying, but didn't ask questions. It was a mistake I would regret.

For one month, the fish and I lived parallel, uneventful lives.

Then, late one evening, Neena's seven-year-old brother Raj sadly said to me, "The water in the fishbowl is cloudy. The fish will die."

"Then tell their mother," I said.

"She's at a sleepover," he replied. "She gave me a note about it to give to you, but I lost it. We need to change the water."

I brought the fish bowl to the kitchen sink, and found the strainer Neena used for holding the fish while she replaced the water.

"The water has to be at room temperature," Raj said.

For a long time, he and I could not agree on when the water had reached room temperature. Finally we agreed and replaced the water.

A bit later, Raj, again looking sad, said, "I can't find the drops."

I had no idea what he was talking about. "Drops?" I asked.

"Drops to correct the pH," he explained. "If we don't correct the pH, the fish will die." He certainly knew more about caring for fish than I did.

We went into Neena's room to try to find the drops.

Neena had arranged her bed at an angle to the wall, forming a triangle.

The only way to reach the other side was to climb over it. I had wondered why her room was set up that way, but had concluded that it was a teenager's whim. There was no harm in it, so I had let it be.

While searching for the drops amidst the clothes, books, and other assorted stuff scattered all over the floor, on top of the desk and in her drawers, I noticed a light emanating from the corner of the room. I didn't want to have to climb over the bed to figure out what it was, so I asked Raj to check it. He jumped over and then promptly jumped back, looking surprised.

"What did you see?" I asked.

"I'm not sure I should tell you," he said.

"I can climb over, too," I said.

"You will be upset."

"I need to know," I said.

"It's a glass tank with a light bulb."

"And?"

"There's a snake in it. The light bulb keeps it warm." He continued to explain, but I screamed, "A snake!" and was out of the room in an instant, pulling Raj along with me. I shut the door behind me.

Grandma heard me scream, and rushed upstairs. "Did you say 'snake?!'" she asked.

"Yes," Raj told her. "In Neena's room, in a glass tank"

She went into her room and shut the door.

We never found those drops.

Neena and Sharad could have managed the situation, but Sharad was out of town, and we had no idea where Neena had gone.

We had to spend night with the snake in our home, our bedroom doors shut tight.

Raj wasn't afraid. "We'll be alright," he said.

The next morning, I looked at the fish. They were swimming peacefully. The lack of pH correction hadn't hurt them.

"I heard the snake hissing all night," Grandma said.

"American snakes don't hiss," I told her, though I knew nothing about American snakes. Then I started to hear hissing too.

Sharad showed up at noon. The moment he stepped into the house, Raj told him about the snake.

Sharad went upstairs, moved the bed, and picked up the snake. Gently putting it on his shoulder, he walked into the kitchen. It was a foot long and black, yellow, and brown.

Grandma and I walked out.

"It's harmless," Sharad insisted.

"Its mere presence bothers me and your mother," I shouted. "Put it back in its tank. When Neena comes home, get rid of it."

I knew my argument was pointless. Sharad and his children love any non-human life form that moves, flies, jumps, creeps, or crawls better than their wife or mother.

Neena arrived a little later. By then the snake had moved out of its tank, and Raj and Sharad were taking turns carrying it on their shoulders. I had given up my plan to yell at Neena.

"How long did you hide the snake?" I asked her.

"Its name is Lucifer," she told me. "I bought it, and then I had to buy fish to feed it. So ever since then, I've had fish."

"What?!" I exclaimed. "You feed those live, cute fish to the snake?"

Photo of a snake resembling Lucifer (via Wikimedia Commons)

"It's 'Lucifer,' Mom! She has a name. I have to feed her fish. That's what she eats."

My ignorance of snake dining habits surprised her.

Finally, the mystery of the disappearing fish had been solved.

I tried to threaten Neena: "I'm not going to help you take care of Lucifer."

"I know what you can and can't do," she said.

"Lucifer must be hungry," she said.

We watched her feed fish to the snake.

As she swallowed, her body developed a swelling, which slowly moved along, away from her head. I couldn't watch the whole operation.

"My son and his children are crazy," Grandma muttered.

Grandma and I soon learned to ignore the snake's presence. We coexisted.

One day, Neena announced, "Lucifer is sick. She's stopped eating."

"She's little," I said, "and eats entire fish. She probably has indigestion." Then I suggested the medicine that my grandfather always turned to for all illnesses: castor oil.

"Tylenol," Raj suggested.

Neena made a face. She went to the pet shop where she'd bought Lucifer. There she bought an ointment, and rubbed it on Lucifer's body. She wore her jacket all day and carried Lucifer in her pockets to keep her warm. Lucifer even went to school with her. No one complained.

But Lucifer refused to eat.

Finally Neena took Lucifer to a vet.

The receptionist asked her, "What color is your pet?"

Neena pulled Lucifer from her pocket, and held her in the receptionist's face.

The woman screamed and jumped. Cats in the waiting room hissed, and dogs barked.

Neena pocketed the snake again.

The commotion brought the vet out, and he took the crazy girl carrying a snake in her pocket into the exam room.

He looked Lucifer over and said, "Lucifer needs to see a specialist."

The next day, a specialist examined her and said, "I have to admit her."

Neena came home crying.

"Will our Blue Cross Blue Shield cover Lucifer?" I muttered.

The next day, Dr. Brown, the specialist, called. He wanted to talk to Neena's father or mother. Sharad spoke with him.

"Lucifer has leukemia," the doctor said. "She needs chemotherapy. The chances of remission are 20 percent. What do you want to do?"

"I need to talk to my daughter," Sharad said.

"I can put her to sleep, if you wish," the doctor offered.

Neena cried and said, "Let her go. Can we get her body and bury it?"

Sharad let her talk to Dr. Brown.

"To put a snake to sleep, we have to cut her," the doctor said. "You taking her body is not a good idea."

Neena consented.

Thus, Lucifer's life, true to her inauspicious name, ended sadly.

Without complaining, I paid the vet's bill.

It was $200.00.

Chapter 18
Kia, Kiska, and others

Kia and Kiska (photo by Philip Shanahan)

When I visit my daughter in Alaska, I have to live with her pets. Over the years, she has had multiple dogs, cats, and other pets.

When her baby was born, I spent six months with the baby and my daughter's two dogs, Kia and Kiska. Kia was a husky-Shepherd mix, white with a black stripe down her back. Kiska was a beautiful purebred Siberian Husky. She had thick white fur and ice-blue eyes. My daughter had rescued both dogs from the pound. When she got them, Kia was a puppy, and Kiska was an adult dog that someone else hadn't been able to keep after a divorce.

Riley

My daughter also had a brown tabby cat named Riley. Riley was a hunter who would wander and hunt whatever he could, bringing home his prey as a present to the family.

The two dogs lived in a doghouse behind the home during the day. They slept in the home at night.

I spent time with the dogs before the baby was born. When I walked them, they pulled me along. Huskies are sled dogs and love to pull. So my walk was effortless: no calories were burned. I could only control them because their collars were attached to a leash that pinched.

When I was alone in the house, if the doorbell rang, they stood guarding me, one to my right and one to my left. Any stranger who saw the dogs promptly stepped back.

As my daughter's due date approached, both dogs seemed to sense that something was about to happen. They were restless.

Before the baby came home, the dogs were allowed to sniff something the baby had worn. When we arrived from the hospital with the baby, the dogs were excited. They were very protective of the baby and refused to sleep in their doghouse. Instead, they would sprawl in the living room or on my daughter's bedroom floor — wherever the baby was. In order to pick up the baby, everyone had to step over the dogs. It was a problem at night when I went up to my daughter's bedroom to pick up the baby so my daughter could sleep. Both Kiska and Kia insisted on walking with me up the stairs and coming into my bedroom. I was afraid I was going to fall. If the doorbell rang, one dog stayed with the baby, and one came to the door. If the baby cried, a dog would herd me to the crib.

The cat, Riley, tolerated the baby, but did not like me. If I was trying to sit in a chair, he would jump up and curl up there to block me. There was a clear hierarchy in the home. The cat was at the top of the pecking order, then my daughter, who could control the dogs, then Kia, then Kiska, followed by my daughter's husband, who is gentle with animals, and tried to negotiate with them. I was an unwanted presence. The cat was unruly and did what he wanted. Kia dominated Kiska, who wasn't very smart. Periodically Kiska ran away. She could dig a tunnel under the fence to escape. We would get in a car and drive around looking for her. She also buried bones in the backyard. At first, the dogs didn't totally trust me with the baby. But as time passed, they relaxed.

After a couple of months, Kia's behavior changed. She stopped eating and stayed in her dog house. Kiska was upset, and ran back and forth from the dog house, whining. She was trying to get Kia to come into the house.

The vet examined her, did a liver biopsy, and diagnosed her with cancer. Everyone was upset.

Even the little baby sensed something was wrong. Soon Kia was gone, put to sleep. Kiska searched for her, looking everywhere, and finally understood. She was lonely and sad. Riley curled up around the tin containing Kia's ashes.

Then the baby noticed Kiska. He giggled when she barked. He would flip over, creep up to her, and pull her fur. She licked him, which I didn't really like, but the others didn't seem to mind. His first word was not Mama or Dada, but "Kih-ka".

Then the little family moved into a bigger home. Kiska adjusted, but Riley hated the move. He disappeared for a few days, and finally was found hiding in a bathroom drawer.

When the baby was six months old, I went home.

When I returned after a few months, Riley had become comfortable in the house. It had two decks, one on each side. He would hunt and leave half-dead voles on the side porch. The voles tossed and turned. I couldn't deal with them. But Kiska did: she ate them. After Riley killed a baby rabbit, my daughter started tying a bell around his neck. That may have warned the birds he was coming, but he continued to kill voles.

At some point, Kiska died, and the family rescued another dog, Kona. She was a husky-greyhound mix, and good at jumping over sofas. She had attachment issues, and bonded to my daughter. If Kona was left alone, she chewed up whatever she could find. In the car, she chewed up a seatbelt. As a result, someone always had to be with her. My daughter's husband kept her at his office during the daytime.

Kona

When their son was ten, my daughter and her husband went away, leaving my grandson and the animals with my husband and me. Even though my grandson was there, Kona was very unhappy, and refused to eat. She sat at the entrance to the garage, waiting for my daughter. Riley was nonchalant and continued on his expeditions, hunting whatever he could. Sometimes my daughter wished an eagle would take him. But that didn't happen.

While I was gone, Riley died, and my daughter acquired three more cats: Serra, who was an outdoor cat, and Lani and Hoku, who were house cats. Lani bonded with Kona the dog. By then, Kona was sick, and would just lie in one place.

Kona and Lani

Lani seemed to sense that Kona wasn't well, and would sit by her side, with her body touching Kona. My daughter took a photo of Lani with Kona. The picture was so touching that a local coffee shop displayed it. When I saw the picture, I realized that animals can be really different. Lani, just like a person, comforted Kona, while the other cats ignored her.

Soon Kona was gone.

Now my daughter has her three cats and a new dog, named Neva — yet another pound pup. Neva had been rescued as a puppy with her mother and the rest of her litter. She is a secure dog — not traumatized like Kona. She is well behaved and doesn't run away. She is protective of my grandson, who is now an adult. If anyone pretends to hurt him, she barks at them.

My daughter also has a gecko, who lives in a glass tank. Every few days, she takes him out and feeds him mango baby food. He also eats crickets, which are sold in a bag. If the bag isn't emptied into the cage properly, crickets hop all over the house, only to be eaten by the cats. It's a regular food chain.

In these many years of watching my daughter's many animals, I've learned some valuable lessons. A secure childhood is important to animals, just like it is to people. If they are deprived of their mother, or abused as a baby, they sustain trauma for life. Adoption into a secure home doesn't totally compensate for an insecure puppyhood. I also learned that animals have distinct personalities. Hoku and Lani, though both from the same litter, have very different personalities.

I still don't like to pet dogs or cats. Neva understands that. She instinctively runs to my husband to greet him, and ignores me. I think as a child, my family's unpredictable dog Tomya traumatized me. That's why, though I like animals, I prefer to observe them from a distance, and don't pet them, don't like to sit with them, and don't like them in my bed.

Even though I've kept at a distance, these animals have enriched my life.

Neva

Chapter 19
Loyal Rascal

It was deep winter. Four feet of snow was piled up wherever it hadn't been shoveled. Our driveway was buried, and the garage door was blocked by snow. We had shoveled enough space to park both cars in the driveway, and carved a path on the sidewalk to get to the front door.

After we went to sleep that night, an additional four inches of snow piled up on top of what we already had.

Sharad and I were both retired and had nowhere to go the next morning. I was fast asleep, but Sharad heard a cat. His knowledge of cats told him that the cat was distressed. He woke up, got dressed, and went out to find it.

He didn't have to go very far. He went out the front door and found a skinny cat on the front porch, yowling pathetically. He decided the cat was hungry. We didn't have cat food. All he could offer was a dish of milk, which the cat lapped up hungrily. Knowing the cat was hungry, Sharad warmed up some leftover rice, and offered it to the cat in a bowl. But even a very hungry feral American cat — unlike cats from India, who eat anything — refused to eat rice.

Sharad picked up his car keys and wallet and drove to a grocery store on unplowed roads . He wouldn't have ventured out for me in that kind of weather, but for an animal, he would do anything. He bought cat food and offered it to the hungry cat. After the cat ate the food, Sharad tried to pick it up and bring it into our house, because it was so cold outside. But the cat fought and scratched him. Sharad left him on the porch. He had breakfast, and went back to the porch afterwards to check if the cat was still around. It had disappeared.

He looked in the backyard next, but the cat was gone.

In the evening, the cat showed up on the front porch, and Sharad fed him again. Sharad realized that the cat was skinny because he must have been starving for days. He thought the cat must be feral. It was treating Sharad like a food source, but was not interested in companionship.

A month went by. The cat showed up for his meals and went away. He allowed Sharad to pet him gently, but would not allow him to pick him up. I warned Sharad that the cat was probably not vaccinated, and that it would be dangerous to try to lift the cat. He ignored my warnings, and fed the cat, petted him, and went on trying to lift him onto his lap. But the cat wouldn't let him.

Sharad named the cat "Bhikya," meaning beggar, because he came to beg for food, but would not come inside the house.

Neighbors noticed, and asked Sharad if he was running a cat shelter. Sharad laughed. When we went away, Sharad asked a neighborhood kid to fill the cat's dish with cat food every day.

When we returned, we discovered that another cat had joined Bhikya. According to Sharad, the new cat was still a kitten. He guessed that even though the kitten wasn't wearing a tag, he belonged to someone. He didn't seem feral like Bhikya. He let Sharad pick him up and pet him.

Cat resembling Rascal (photo via Wikimedia Commons)

As time passed, we noticed that Bikya and the kitten had a peculiar relationship. The kitten respected Bhikya. He arrived for lunch at the same time as Bhikya. But he waited for Bhikya to arrive and eat before he ate leftovers. Bhikya had a certain spot on the steps where he would sit. The kitten would sit there until Bikya arrived. Then he promptly vacated Bhikya's place. The kitten waited to drink water until Bhikya drank. Sharad said that the kitten was afraid of Bhikya, who was bigger, and would beat him in a fight. I didn't doubt Sharad, because I could see how the kitten behaved. Sharad named him Rascal.

Soon after we came back from a vacation, Bhikya started to lose weight. Sharad bought salmon for him, cooked it, and fed him. But he lost some of his fur and more weight. For a change, he hung around the front porch, and was lethargic. Then Sharad noticed he had a few bumps. He decided that Bhikya needed help. He called a veterinarian, who arrived with a cage. The moment Bhikya saw the vet, he tried to run, but he was too weak. The veterinarian caught him by the scruff of his neck, and locked him in a cage.

Rascal was watching, loudly hissing and growling. When the veterinarian put the cage down, Rascal jumped on top of it, and wouldn't let the vet touch it. He tried to scratch the vet's arms. The vet picked Rascal up by the scruff of his neck. With his other hand, he carried the cage to his car. He put the cage in the car, tossed Rascal in our yard, and drove away. Not wanting to face Rascal, we locked ourselves in the house.

The next day, we learned that Bhikya had advanced cancer. The vet asked our permission to put him to sleep.

That day, Rascal showed up at lunch time. When Sharad tried to pick him up, he hissed and scratched him. Refusing the food that was offered, Rascal ran away.

He never visited again. He never forgave Sharad for how he mistreated Bhikya.

Chapter 20
Mini animal dramas

One early morning in the summer, I walked into the kitchen and noticed a plastic square box on top of the radiator. Someone had punched holes in the cover. Without thinking, I opened it. Inside, on a bed of green leaves, were a large number of caterpillars, worms, and inchworms. They were crawling, creeping or inching along. Some were green, others were black or white or beige. Some were really hairy. A few were lying curled at the bottom, others were climbing the smooth surface of the plastic box, and one was upside down on the box cover.

I screamed, threw the box on the kitchen floor, and ran out. I must have screamed loudly because the entire family, except Raj, who was asleep, came running.

"Worms!" I screamed at them.

"What? Are you dreaming?" Sharad asked.

"My worms!" Neena yelled, and ran into the kitchen.

Tearfully, she scrambled to pick up the worms that were crawling on the kitchen floor. Sharad and Veena started to help her.

Sharad said to Neena, "You should know better than to leave your worm collection in the kitchen. You know what your mother is like."

Neena conceded her mistake. "The box was in my room," she said. "Yesterday I brought it down to show the worms to my friends, and I forgot it in the kitchen."

Bravely I stood in the kitchen door and watched the scene. I remembered that my mother had told me that if you touch a caterpillar, you develop a rash. Neena and the rest of the family were picking up caterpillars with their fingers. They were fine: no rash.

They collected all the worms they could find and put them in the box. The box was moved to Neena's room and set on top of a piece of paper that said, "Worms inside." The sign was for the benefit of babysitters and visiting friends.

Over the next few days, I imagined that something creepy-crawly was on me. My fear wasn't irrational. A few worms had escaped and were hiding in the kitchen. Periodically, one would appear. When I saw one, I screamed and ran away. After a week, they were all gone from the kitchen — either into the box, or dead in an invisible kitchen crack.

* * * *

Neena also loved mice, dead or alive. She could catch a live mouse in a bottle when she was six years old. She must've inherited the skill of catching live mice from an ancestor, because even Sharad cannot catch a mouse.

There were many pet cats wandering around in our neighborhood. They killed mice. In India, cats kill mice and eat them. Well-fed American cats kill mice just for fun and leave them around.

The dead mice Neena imported into her room and hid in drawers posed a major problem. The smell didn't seem to bother her. But it was an issue for the rest of us. Nobody wanted to find a smelly dead mouse — much less pick it up to dispose of it. Babysitters were freaked out by the smell, and refused to set foot in Neena's room.

Neena's argument was, "A dead mouse is still a mouse." Eventually, I convinced her to bury the dead mice like dead people. She started burying them, and the problem was resolved.

* * * *

Mittens the cat belonged to a neighbor, but lived in our home. He would arrive early in the morning and hang around until the girls went to school. Someone, not me, fed him. Whoever was the last one to leave had to kick him out, because I didn't want to have to keep a kitty litter box in the house. I also didn't want this uninvited guest to move in permanently.

When Mittens was at our house and had to go to the bathroom, he would scratch at our front door, and someone would let him out. He would then go over to his owners' house and meow and scratch at the front door. If the owners were home, they let him in. When they weren't, he would stand there for a while, and then I don't know how he resolved the issue. But resolve it he did, and returned to our home.

He must have had a clock in his brain. He would show up just about the time the girls got home from school. He stayed until we had our supper, and someone, not me, fed him cat food. After the girls went to bed, I would kick him out of the house.

He always returned the next morning.

One day, he was standing in front of his owners' house, meowing and pacing back and forth with an arched back. The girls noticed, and started to demand that we keep a kitty litter box in our home. I firmly refused. The argument went on for a few days.

Then I noticed that many cats were visiting our backyard. Wondering why, I searched the slope where we had many untended bushes. There I found a box filled with sand. I realized the girls had set it up there for Mittens, and that other cats had discovered it and were using it, too. Upset, I got rid of the box. But then I started to find boxes with sand in different locations around the yard. Finally I gave up.

* * * *

Raj was growing up. He loved the fish in the fish tanks at Chinese restaurants, and at the homes of friends, who had pretty, colorful fish.

I bought a fish, had the salesman cut it, and cooked it. That didn't seem to bother Raj. Then his grandmother came to stay with us. She loved fish. But she wished to cut the fish she cooked herself. I bought a whole fish so she could cut it the way she wanted. Raj was upset, and cried.

111

His argument was, "So what if the fish is dead? It's still a fish." It reminded me of Neena's argument about dead mice.

I tried instructing the salesman about how to cut a fish the way grandma liked it. He tried, but grandma wasn't happy. She was forced to cook fish that had been cut by the salesman because her beloved grandson cried.

* * * *

Where we live in Florida there are numerous geckos. They live everywhere — under bricks, stones, and trees. I see them in parking lots and on sidewalks.

To our grandchildren visiting from New York, geckos are a novelty. They run with their tails curled, and they can change colors. The grandchildren think they're hilarious.

When the grandchildren visit, we take them to a park. They see so many geckos there that they call it a gecko park. Once, when they were visiting, Sharad caught some geckos and put them on the children's arms. Neither the children nor the geckos appreciated it. The children stood still, afraid that the geckos would crawl around on them. The geckos stood still, too. I complained, and finally Sharad picked them up and put them back on the ground. The geckos ran away as fast as they could.

After Sharad got rid of the geckos, I cleaned the children's arms with hand sanitizer. I tried to clean Sharad's arms, but he refused.

Since then, every time Sharad goes near a gecko, he develops a rash. If we are seated outdoors at a restaurant, or in a garden or park, Sharad develops a rash if geckos are close by. I call the phenomenon "revenge of the geckos."

He never touches geckos now.

* * * *

I don't remember how or why Brownie the hamster arrived in our home. I do remember setting aside my opposition to importing pets into the house when he arrived.

I hadn't realized that having Brownie would mean having a cage with a squeaky metal wheel that Brownie would constantly ride, creating a racket. Due to the racket, his cage had to be in the living room. Also because of the racket, we never had peace in the living room.

Not only that, but the wood shavings — or whatever it was at the bottom of the cage — smelled. The rest of the family had no issue with the smell, but I did. Having consented to import Brownie, I just had to learn to live with the racket and the smell.

Mittens the cat was seriously interested in Brownie. He sat by the cage, licking his lips. To protect Brownie from Mittens, heavy books were set on top of the cage.

There was another complication. To keep Brownie healthy, he had to be set free to run around for at least half an hour each day. Being a rodent, he had to be watched constantly while he was free. I had a friend who told me her children's hamster had disappeared during free time. They were wondering where it had gone when they started to find burrows in the upholstered furniture and mattresses. They couldn't find the hamster, but the number of burrows increased. The set-free hamster had done what rodents do. Finally they managed to catch the hamster, but they had to replace their furniture.

I warned the girls to watch Brownie carefully while he was free because Mittens was waiting to hunt him, and because Brownie could disappear like my friend's hamster.

The girls were careful. Before setting Brownie free, they had to make sure Mittens wasn't in the house. They would search the house, find him, and put him out. He waited outside for a chance to sneak back in. So they had to watch the door. Brownie loved to waddle under furniture, and he was very quick. The girls had to crawl behind him, and drag him back out when he went under the sofa.

I liked to watch Brownie waddle, shaking his behind.

Unfortunately, Brownie didn't last very long. One morning, I didn't hear the racket from his wheel. Soon Veena noticed that he was lying still at the bottom of his cage. Sharad looked at him, and said that his back and legs were paralyzed.

Off Sharad and Veena went to the vet, Sharad missing his work, and Veena missing school. I knew that was the end of Brownie, but I didn't say a word. When they returned, Veena was crying. The vet had told them that Brownie's back was broken. He said that hamsters forget how fast they're rotating the wheel, and fall and break their backs. There was no treatment. Brownie could have died naturally if left alone. The vet offered to end Brownie's misery. Sharad told me that the vet talked to Veena, and totally ignored him, which was good. The vet let Veena make the decision to end Brownie's life.

The girls and Mittens missed Brownie. Mittens stood in the living room looking at the empty cage. The living room was peaceful again.

I had learned a lesson. I donated the glass cage to a friend, and decided never to import a rodent into the house again.

After Brownie was gone, the girls didn't ask for another rodent — like the gerbil they had once wanted. I think they learned a lesson, too. Brownie's free time cut into their free time. They spent an hour searching for Mittens, putting him out, watching Brownie, and dragging him out of the spaces he crawled into. They learned that a cat and a rodent cannot coexist.

* * * *

Such little dramas involving animals were constantly playing out in our home. I had to learn to live with them.

Acknowledgements

I could not have completed this book without help from Sage Stossel, who edited it, helped me choose photographs, and addressed other details.

I must also thank illustrator Amit Kaikini for his striking cover design, his nicely done drawings of the animal world, and for his patience.

I would also like to thank many friends, including Dr. Dhimant Patel, Neela Inamdar, Rajashree Palkar, Neel Palkar, Nandini Bhide, Vaishali Shukla, Sheela Sogal, Gambhirwala Neena, and Rekha Keluskar, who contributed pictures. And my family, who read early drafts of the book and contributed memories and photos.

Without all of you I could not have written this book. Thank you all.

Lalita Gandbhir is the author of the family memoir *Tales Across Time: My family's life in India, 1846 to 1990*, and the novel *For Homeland: A Sikh Refugee Story*. The original Marathi version of *For Homeland*, "Dahashatwadachi Katha," published by Granthali Prakashan, was awarded the 2003-2004 Maharashtra Government Award for Fiction. Her fiction, poetry, and non-fiction have been published in India, Canada and the United States, both in Marathi and in English, in such venues as *The South Asian Review, Ekata, Weber Studies, Her Mother's Ashes*, and *The Massachusetts Review*. A former physician, she now lives in Singer Island, Florida with her husband.

Some of these articles have been previously published in Marathi in Ekata *magazine, based in Toronto, Canada and* Antaraal, *in New Jersey.*

Also by Lalita Gandbhir:

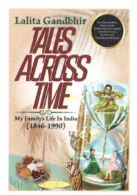

Tales Across Time: My Family's Life in India, 1846-1990 (*published in 2022 by Vithal Publications*)

Lalita Gandbhir, who was born in 1938 and grew up in Pune, India, vividly and insightfully describes her family's life, spanning a period from her great-grandfather's generation to the recent past. She addresses everything from issues of caste to birthing and parenting practices to arranged marriages, family living arrangements, and customs. She covers such memorable events as the influenza pandemic of 1918, her family's periodic retreat into the jungle during epidemics of plague, ghosts that lived among people, mob attacks near her family's bungalow following the assassination of Mahatma Gandhi, and her own experience as a young child during World War II.

For Homeland: A Sikh Refugee Story (*published in 2019 by Vithal Publications*)

The novel *For Homeland* is the epic saga of a Sikh family whose lives are violently disrupted and their loyalties divided by the partition of British India in the 1940s, and again by the Sikh community's struggle for a separate nation of Khalistan in the 1980s.
Available via Amazon in the United States ($9.99), Canada, the United Kingdom, Australia, India, and elsewhere.

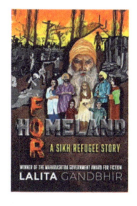

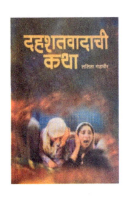

Dahashtwadachi Katha (*published in 2003 by Granthali Prakashan*)

Written in Gandbhir's native Marathi, the novel *Dahashtwadachi Katha* was the winner of the Maharashtra Government fiction award for 2003. (Gandbhir's 2019 novel *For Homeland* is an edited, English-language version of this book).

Short story collections:

Paxi Jay Deshantara (*published in 1993 by Utkasha Prakashan*).

Pashimgandha (*published in 1989 by Nihara Prakashan*)

Tarevrachi Kasarat (*published in 1987 by Shrividya Prakashan*)

Article Collection:

Pashupremiyanchya Duniyet (*published in 1991 by Rashmi Prakashan*)

Coming Soon:

Glacier Princess
A children's picture book set in Alaska.

Made in the USA
Coppell, TX
21 March 2023